Praise for *The Im*

"We all need cheerleaders. *The Impossible Kid* will
parent. Raising a child who loves God is becomi
best way to learn something is to experience it.
roller coaster with smiles and laughter to sniffles ;
how to laugh at yourself, have fun, and enjoy you
struggles as a mom. Each page has new surprises,
at the end of each chapter. A great read from cover to cover as you are saying, *Yes! Exactly!
I know just what you mean!"*

—**Gary Smalley**, author of *Guarding Your Child's Heart*

"Lucille Williams is the real deal! She writes with amazing authenticity, practicality, and
a fun-loving sense of humor. Reading this book (and her other books) is like sitting with
a good friend over coffee sprinkled with important 'truth bombs' and a lot of laughs. I
always encourage the HomeWord audience to pick up her books. And with this book, her
daughter Monica chimes in at every chapter with the style of fun, authenticity, and truth."

—**Jim Burns**, PhD, President, HomeWord, author of *Doing Life With Your
Adult Children: Keep Your Mouth Shut and the Welcome Mat Out!*

"Lucille Williams and her daughter Monica take us on an exciting adventure into the
challenging world of parenting. Captivating stories will keep you laughing, crying, and
turning pages to find a healthy dose of practical guidance, hilarious antidotes, and the
reminder that we are all God's kids. Some of us are just bigger than others."

—**Claudia Mitchell**, Women's Minister, Sherwood Oaks Christian Church,
Bloomington, Indiana, and coauthor of *One Girl Can Change the World*

"Lucille Williams has painted the pages of this book with all of her personality, the same
personality that is so endearing as she ministers in the children's ministry at Shepherd
Church in Porter Ranch, California. She writes with authenticity and a realness that is
not only disarming but engaging. You can't help but laugh and cry at the stories she shares.
She has encapsulated what it means to parent your children, even with the ups and downs,
with the joy of the Lord. A great and encouraging read!"

—**Phil Allen**, Founder & Pastor at Own Your Faith Ministries, California

"I have always believed you can't really do parenting *to* a child; you do it *with* a child. In
other words, just as much as a parent shapes the future of a child, the child shapes the
future of a parent. As I read this book by Lucille, I am refreshed by a parenting book that
is not written about children but *with* children! The wisdom and authenticity of Lucille
coupled with the responses and realizations of Monica are truly some of the most unique
and clever parenting insights I have read in years."

—**Todd Clark**, Pastor, and Senior Associate, Slingshot Group

"It's very refreshing to read a book where both mom and daughter share the good, the bad,
and the ugly of parenting. Let's keep it real, people! Lucille and Monica do a great job
sharing their triumphs and tough times. Full of scripture and encouragement, Lucille tells
how she cried out time and time again to the Lord, and reminds us that this is what we
too must do for successful parenting. If your kids didn't come with instructions, consider
this your powerful parenting play book."

—**Annett Davis**, professional beach volleyball player,
2000 Olympian, pastor's wife, and mother of two

"I can relate to the book. I have a daughter who is just like the one portrayed here. She is the joy of my life, but I welcome any sound advice from people like Lucille Williams. She has done a great job on laying it out in a humorous and enjoyable fashion."

–**Rick Kyle**, Teaching Pastor, The Hills Church in Evansville

"There is certainly no such thing as a perfect parent or a perfect child, but Lucille Williams shows you how to find the humor and joy in parenting the Lord's way. You will laugh and cry as you glean from the godly wisdom shared in *The Impossible Kid* through exploring the real issues that moms and dads face today. And while every child is unique and sure to keep us on our toes, this book reveals that being a perfectly content parent is truly possible."

–**Dudley C. Rutherford**, Senior Pastor Shepherd Church

"Lucille Williams offers biblically-based advice and wisdom on parenting mixed with a very healthy dose of humor and encouragement. Her book is sure to be a valuable resource for parents who desire to joyfully honor God as they raise their children!"

–**Renee Rutherford**, wife of Senior Pastor Shepherd Church,
Porter Ranch, California, and mother of three

"Sometimes you see the title and author of a book, and even before you read the first page you think to yourself, *Yeah, this is going to be good.* That is the case with Lucille Williams and her new book on parenting. She is a woman who has had not only an incredible amount of personal experience with being a mother, but she is also someone who has walked alongside many other mothers, gaining additional experience as a mentor and a friend. As a husband whose household consists of a wife, two teenage daughters, and a female golden retriever, this book is an answer to prayer."

–**Tim Winters**, Executive Pastor of Shepherd Church, Porter Ranch, California

"As a mother of two preteen boys, I was so blessed by Lucille Williams' stories and antidotes in *The Impossible Kid.* You will feel encouraged by the way she is able to combine the challenges of motherhood with God's specific promise to that area. I was able to identify with many of her issues (and attitudes) on parenting. Other times I was spurred into action—having to put the book down and go make things right with my kids. This book is for parents at all stages of parenting who seek some lighthearted, yet sound godly advice from a mom who's been there."

–**Kim Wynott**, mother of two boys, including child star Ryan
Wynott from ABC's *FlashForward* and NBC's *The Cape*

"To write a book on raising a strong-willed child *with* that strong-willed child is a bold move! You can only imagine the 'vigorous' editing process, and we, the readers, are the beneficiaries. The pious platitudes and easy answers are ousted by the emotional roller coaster of reality, accompanied by laughter, tears, and the trauma of parenting."

–**Mark E. Moore**, PhD. Teaching Pastor of Christ's Church of the Valley, and author
of *Core 52: A Fifteen-Minute Daily Guide to Build Your Bible IQ in a Year*

"Lucille is vulnerable, honest, and raw with you about her journey as a mom. She won't shame you, but encourage you in your calling from God to be a mom."

–**Kyle Idleman**, Pastor of Southeast Christian Church,
and author of *Not a Fan* and *Don't Give Up*

The Impossible Kid

Parenting a
STRONG-WILLED CHILD
with Love and Grace

LUCILLE WILLIAMS
with Monica Welch
(Lucille's own Impossible Kid)

BARBOUR
PUBLISHING

Cover Art: Tanja Varcelija, Advocate Art, Inc.

Published in association with the literary agency of Credo Communications, LLC, Grand Rapids, Michigan, www.credocommunications.net.

Published by Barbour Publishing, Inc., 1810 Barbour Drive, Uhrichsville, Ohio 44683, www.barbourbooks.com

Our mission is to inspire the world with the life-changing message of the Bible.

 Member of the
Evangelical Christian
Publishers Association

Printed in the United States of America.

Introduction

What's important? What really matters to you? Within minutes of the birth of my first child, I couldn't think of anything more important to do with my life than raise my family. I knew I wanted to raise a child who would love and depend on God. I knew I wanted to shelter her from harm. I wanted her to become a productive member of society, one that didn't live off the system or, even worse, *in* the system. I wanted her to one day be a woman of character and integrity. I knew what my aim was, but I had no idea how and if I would ever hit the target.

What I did not know was how hard it would be. I did not know how this cute little helpless child would pull, tear, and rip open my heart and send me into tailspins, shaking my head and asking God, "Okay, what next?"

When a mother's journey begins, one is venturing into the unknown. It's hard to imagine what this tiny little baby will be as an adult. My journey was difficult, heart-wrenching, laborious and yet joyful, worth every tear and strife. My child seemed impossible to me, but God chose me to be the mother of this *impossible* child. And what we deem impossible, God makes possible (Luke 18:27).

The idea to write this book came from my daughter. When Monica was seventeen, with her "I can conquer the world" outlook, she said, "Write a book about raising me. You always say I was your hardest. Then at the end of every chapter, I'll write what I think, my perspective." I have to admit that at first I thought it was a crazy idea, but the more I thought about it, the more I liked it. And now that she's a mom of *an impossible kid*, it seemed that this was the perfect time for a book such as this.

So, there you have it—the birth of our mother-daughter story. Everyone has a story. This is our story. This is my parenting story. Perhaps you will see your own story as you wander through these pages.

And Mom, thank you for picking up this book, and thank you for all you do—it matters.

Chapter One

_____

"Nothing will be impossible with God."
LUKE 1:37

It was Monica's first day of high school. I sat in the driver's seat in our driveway waiting for her to get in my car. She was nervous. I was nervous for her. Watching her hustle to the car, I thought to myself how beautiful she was with her long, flowing blonde hair; gorgeous green eyes; and a new outfit—red button-up collared shirt and jeans. I was so proud of her. She had grown into such a lovely young lady. But as she got in the car and sat down, her shirt raised and... I could see her skin! I could see the side of her gorgeous bod! I screeched, "Oh my gosh! [*gasp*] I see skin! Look at all this skin! You look like a slut."

She said, "Mom, it's not that bad."

I put the car in reverse and pulled out of the driveway; we couldn't risk her being late. When she got out of the car, I said my standard "I love you. Have a good day," but loving mom was lost at "You look like a slut." Instead of endearment and encouragement, she got fearful, judgmental, crazy mom.

Not my finest mom moment—not even close.

Once on campus, Monica found a friend from church youth group and asked, "Ashley, do I look okay?" Her sweet friend not only told her she looked great but asked one of the boys to chime in and compliment Monica on how she looked.

Mom bombs—friend saves.

When Monica told me how much that hurt her, my response was, "Honey, I am so sorry. That was a terrible thing for me to have done. Please forgive me." She forgave me. And then we laughed. I realized the shirt wasn't any big deal and a little side skin wasn't scandalous at all. We laugh more now, but it grieves me even today, and I wish I could have a do-over on that skin-filled, grace-absent day. Why didn't I say, "Sweetheart, you look so pretty, and I'm so proud of you"? Why? What went wrong? I allowed my fears to take over and spill onto her. That's the thing as a mom, the good as well as the bad spills over.

I'm sure all three of my kids have lasting side effects from many of my not-so-perfect parenting moments. My shortcomings were continually in my face. I'd pray a regular prayer of "Lord, I know I'm falling short as a mom. Please fill in the gaps where I am lacking." My mantra became "I know I'm messing up my kids, but I'll pay for their therapy."

Well, now that my kids are adults, my mantra is "Sorry, guys, I'm paying for *my own* therapy, and you can pay for yours. Which I highly recommend because I know you need it—I was your mom."

As you've probably already figured out, there will be no *Mom Shaming* in the pages that follow. We need to cheer for and support one another with no judgment. Life is hard.

Growing is hard. Being a parent is almost impossible. I learned early on that I had to cling to God and be open to learning and growing as a person. Even today, now that I'm a grandmother, I'm still "working my life out" and learning. All we can do is try to grow through our pain and mistakes—and not judge ourselves in the process. Sometimes it's most difficult to extend grace to ourselves.

I start with this story as my way of saying please have grace with yourself. And give yourself a break! Being a mom, in my opinion, is the most difficult calling you'll ever have. Our kids have a way of pushing us to our outermost limits and then back around again, and again, and again. They have a way of bringing out what is deeply buried inside of us. Sometimes ugly emotions rise to the surface, and we think *What is this and what am I supposed to do with it?* I felt those difficult feelings throughout my parenting journey. You may be feeling some yourself. We can grow. We can change. We can apologize. And we can love ourselves and our families in the process.

Now that that's out of the way, allow me to take you back to the beginning.

THE BEGINNING

I couldn't sleep. All I could do was cry, weeping because I was scared that I was making a wrong decision. Feelings of certainty were nowhere to be found, but I longed for them. At nineteen years old, I had much growing up to do. It was the night before my wedding day.

I was in my sister's room because my room had long been cleaned out and refurnished; since I was living with my "beloved," there was no reason for my parents to leave my room intact. When my grandmother came into town for the wedding, sharing a room with my younger sister was the logical choice. *Grandma must not know that Lucille is living with her boyfriend.* We tried to put on a ruse. When Grandma returned home to New Jersey, she told the family, "Do they think I'm stupid? She wasn't living there! None of her things were there! None of her clothes were there! What am I, stupid?"

Sorry, Grandma. We tried.

My sister, the sixteen-year-old maid of honor, did her best to console the crying bride to no avail.

"Why are you crying?" she questioned.

"Because I'm scared," I answered through my streaming tears.

"Then why are you marrying him?" she asked.

"Because I love him."

I love him. It's the answer to everything when you're nineteen. For me, it wasn't just my answer; it was my reason for making one of the biggest decisions of my life. I was young, naive, and desperate for someone to love me. And there I was, on the eve of my wedding, agonizing over whether I was making a mistake. Truthfully, I felt like I *was* making a mistake, but I also knew I wouldn't back out, and this was the reason for my tears.

The wedding day was supposed to be happy. It was supposed to be perfect. Instead, we got into an argument over the phone. My soon-to-be brother-in-law got on the phone to try to ease the tension—or, more accurately, the yelling. I told him, "I am not going to marry him! He's a jerk! Did you hear what he said to me?!"

But later that day, we did take a walk down the aisle. My brother-in-law somehow got us to resolve our fight, only the first of many more to come. And that was how our family started.

Five years into the battle—I mean *marriage*—our first child was born. I was in no way ready to raise a child. I had not grown up myself. Being emotionally immature, ignorant about life, stubborn, antagonistic, self-centered, and completely self-consumed, I was not going to be awarded "Mother of the Year." Dealing with a lot of my own pain and emotional struggles from my past left me ill-equipped to deal with life in a healthy way, let alone raise a child.

Nonetheless, after Mike and I had been married for just over four years, we decided to begin trying for a baby. This was going to be a huge adjustment for us, because I was in deep pursuit of an acting career. A better way to put it would be obsessed. I was *obsessed* with pursuing my career and had taken a job as a food server so that I could be free for auditions. This was my dream since I was a child, and nothing was going to get in my way, not even my husband. It was my search for significance, and I was good at it. I got to pretend to be someone else. When you don't like being you, acting is a rush. My talent agent was sending me out regularly for auditions, and I spent way too much money taking acting classes, which were sometimes late at night. And I'm embarrassed to admit, I enjoyed the attention I received from other men in the process. Can you say "rocky marriage"? We were like a bomb waiting to explode.

Balance was something God would teach me later. We made the decision that I would be a stay-at-home mom. Many women successfully balance kids and career, and if that's you, I take my hat off to you. I knew I did not have the capacity to do both; I could hardly hold my life together without children. It wasn't an easy decision, though. I felt like I was giving up and giving away everything I ever dreamed of, and it meant sacrificing my significance and worth.

After getting pregnant, nighttime felt like Christmas Eve. I'd be wide awake because I was so excited about being a mom, never mind it would take nine months. Most nights my anticipation would win out over sleep, and I'd read my Bible. Mike was excited too, but he was sleeping fine. *A baby is coming; how can he sleep?* I think the anticipation was also mixed with a lot of anxiety and fear about becoming a mom.

Going to my Bible felt urgent. Mike and I had become Christians just before getting pregnant. In hindsight, God was preparing me for His plan, and those late nights were my classroom. " 'For I know the plans that I have for you,' declares the LORD, "plans for prosperity and not for disaster, to give you a future and a hope' " (Jeremiah 29:11). God's plan for us is always better than our plan. I just needed to surrender my agenda and dreams for God's perfect design, and He would make all things beautiful in His time. As the nights went by, I'd read and spend time with God.

My first mom-task while waiting for the baby was to wash the baby clothes. I threw everything in the washer without separating a thing. . .and turned everything pink. *I knew it, I knew it, I'm going to be a terrible mom—I can't even wash the baby clothes right.* This only added to my already brewing anxiety.

Weeks after my due date, I finally went into labor. After having contractions through the day and into the night, along with medication to increase my labor, my body was still not dilating. As my doctor sat in a room across the hall, I frantically screamed, "Get the doctor!" while he and my husband exchanged nods.

The nurse came in, and I heard my husband whisper, "Why is she bleeding?"

"I'm bleeding?" I yelled. "Why am I bleeding?"

My doctor rushed in and told my husband I needed an emergency c-section. I was hemorrhaging. The hospital staff called in the assisting surgeon, but he got into a car accident on the way to the hospital. Suddenly, everyone else was frantic while I lay there paralyzed with fear. My doctor was roaring orders, commanding the staff while on the phone trying to find another surgeon. "That guy will *never* work with me again," we heard the doctor say. "I don't care that he got into an accident; you get here!"

An assisting surgeon arrived, and our Monica was born. Not exactly the birth story I had dreamed of during all those sleepless nights, but once she was in my arms, she was the most beautiful thing I had ever seen. Life changed. Each day started with a different view of the world. Each decision affected not just my life but also the life of my child. I couldn't be selfish anymore. Life suddenly became scarier and significantly more intense.

While in the hospital, I felt protected. There were nurses ready to help me at the push of a button. But the thought of going home terrified me. I didn't feel like an adult. How could I raise a child? I couldn't even wash the baby clothes right. *Please don't send me home with this baby*, I thought.

I was in no way emotionally ready to go home, but it was

time. The nurse arrived with my wheelchair of terror. The baby was bundled up in her new going-home outfit; my husband and mother were excited; and I was crying so hard, I could hardly breathe.

The nurse and my husband helped me into the wheelchair. Beautiful little Monica was placed in my lap. *Wait! I don't think I can do this. Oh no, here we go. What am I going to do? I do not know how to be a mom!* I was so scared. As I was wheeled out of my hospital room and down the hall, the tears rapidly flew down my face. From the elevator all the way to the hospital lobby, my cries did not subside. How embarrassing! I can only imagine what the people watching were thinking: *Here is this new mom holding her baby going home. How sweet. Ah, look at that, what a nice picture. No, wait! That young mother is sobbing like a baby. What's the matter with her? Is there something wrong with that perfect-looking little baby? The baby looks normal. What's the deal with that young mother? What's her problem? Is the baby sick or something?*

Even as we left the hospital through the lobby doors, I was still weeping. We got into our red Ford Mustang GT—a real family car. I guess we were young, scared, *and* stupid. Mike was driving; my mom sat in the front; and the sobbing new mother was in the back with the baby in her car seat. I cried all the way home, all throughout the forty-five minute drive. My husband and mother asked me why I was crying. All I could muster through my sobs was "I'm scared."

It was one thing to make a mess of my life, but now to potentially mess up my child's life? Well, it was too much for me to endure... or so I thought. I had already made a disaster of my life, which included a marriage that in no way could have been described as healthy. I was petrified I would pass on all my mistakes and destroy Monica's life. I didn't want her to experience the things I had: the loneliness, the pain, the emptiness, the hopelessness.

How would I protect her from all the difficulties and sorrows this life offers? She was at the start of a long journey, and I was her guide. I was so unequipped, so ignorant, and so uninformed. Even though I had spent hours reading baby books, made the painful decision to stay home, and had a room ready and waiting for her, it didn't ease any of my fears or despair. I didn't know how to be a mom. I didn't even know how to be an adult yet. The desperation was crippling.

Finally, we made it home. Home was a small townhouse located on the third floor in a bad neighborhood riddled with drugs and prostitutes. To describe it better, I'll tell you a little story. One day I was walking our dog, and it was the middle of the day. I was wearing jeans and a sweatshirt. This elderly man with no teeth asked me if I was "working." I thought he wanted me to walk his dog. My husband had to explain to me what he was really asking. I told you I was naive. It was not the best place to raise a child, but it was home.

The overflow of terror and tears gradually turned into a state of numbness. We were home, but our home was now changed forever. I was changed forever. I was a mom.

BEING PRESENT

Desperate, feeling alone and confused, spending time with God every day sustained me. I was about to learn how to be a mom, and the God of all wisdom and understanding would be my Teacher. He would be my Wonderful Counselor (Isaiah

9:6) and my Helper (Hebrews 13:6).

As I did my best to focus on my husband and my baby, not only did I quit my job, I also gave up the pursuit of acting. I put to rest a dream, but God had something far better for me. God always wants to give us what's best. "Now to Him who is able to do far more abundantly beyond all that we ask or think, according to the power that works within us" (Ephesians 3:20).

The world will tell you that you can have it all. Looking back, now that my kids are all adults, did I make a mistake to give up so much? This is a question I've been wrestling with since the start of this chapter. Do I really believe God gave me more than I could ever hope for?

These thoughts stopped me for a while. I first had to get gut-check honest with myself so that I could be completely transparent and honest with you. As I was mulling over and deep in my "Did I really do the best thing?" vortex, my son asked me to spend time with him. As we hung out and talked, my answer suddenly couldn't have been any clearer. With tears rolling down my face, I realized that, *yes*, God did give me "abundantly beyond" in all three of my adult children.

My oldest allows me to share in her parenting journey and do life with her kids and family. My middle son lives in another state but calls often and invites me to visit. He'll say after a few months, "When are you coming, Mom?" And my youngest—the one who prompted my detour from writing to hang out with him—we talked for over three hours that day.

I wouldn't change the relationship I have with my kids for anything. Not status, not fame, not fortune, *not anything*. I was a present mom. I didn't miss it. I didn't miss their growing-up years. I chose to show up. I wasn't anywhere near perfect, and I made oh so many mistakes—but I was there. I showed up. Showing up is one of the best things you can do for your child.

Do you know the song "Cat's in the Cradle" by Harry Chapin from 1974, where a father has no time for his son, and then, once the son is grown, he doesn't have time for his father? There's such profound truth there.

The first step to a lasting and impactful relationship with your child is—you show up! That's what you do. Be there for your child. Be present. Struggle with them. Cry with them. Learn with them. Grow with them. Stay engaged.

So many things keep us busy and out of touch with our children, and some parents check out when it gets tough. We need to fight for time with them. Don't ever underestimate your presence and love in your child's life. It's not about knowing all the answers—I never did—it's about showing up.

EMBRACE WEAKNESSES

And He has said to me, "My grace is sufficient for you, for power is perfected in weakness." Most gladly, therefore, I will rather boast about my weaknesses, so that the power of Christ may dwell in me.
2 Corinthians 12:9

What do you do with a child who pops out of the womb a leader? A child who is so strong she thinks she can rule the world and easily rule you? How do you raise a child who wants to violate every boundary, every rule, just because it's there? Pray? Cry? Laugh? Agonize? Yes, yes, yes. . . If you are shouting, "Yup, that's my kid!" then, sister, I'm sending you a hug. I've raised a child like that, and it was downright scary at times.

But here's the hidden blessing: the advantage of "impossible" children is that when they stand for what they believe in, nothing can push them off their foundation. Often, with guidance and a lot of prayer, "impossible" children turn into leaders for Jesus Christ. If I could raise one, so can you!

I often felt like I had no idea what I was doing and would sometimes entertain thoughts of one of my kids ending up on the side of a road with a blanket and a beer can. If you can relate to this, you've come to the right place. One of the hardest things about parenting is feeling like you are not good enough or are doing it wrong. No one does parenting perfectly. Even the perfect parent wouldn't be the perfect parent—there's no such thing. Listen to what famous American psychologist Carl R. Rogers is quoted as saying: "What I am is good enough if I could only be it openly." As a parent, "good enough" is enough because being perfect isn't good enough. We need to lean on grace—grace for our children and grace for us. All we can do is our best at the time.

What is the seemingly impossible parenting challenge you face today? Embrace it, and acknowledge that God is molding you along with your child. Often our largest obstacles become our most celebrated successes. Always remember, God chose you to be the parent for your child. Whatever you feel your weaknesses are, God chose you. Call on Him. You are not doing this alone; God is there for you. Ask Him for wisdom: "But if any of you lacks wisdom, let him ask of God, who gives to all generously and without reproach, and it will be given to him" (James 1:5).

Impossible kids do not have to be impossible to raise. Yes, they can be obstinate, disagreeable, strong-spirited, stubborn, and aggressive; and you can still have a great relationship with them. I will show you how you can leverage this type of personality and come out victorious. And the teen years? They don't have to be as bad as you think—you can actually enjoy your kids during this season. Today Monica is a stay-at-home mom, married to a pastor, put herself through college earning a bachelor's degree in journalism, and was the communications director at a megachurch—having been on staff for ten years. She's a mother who loves her children, loves the people around her, and gives grace freely. She never backs down and always sticks up for others.

Together we can make the impossible possible.

BUILDING OUR HOUSE

I had this concept that motherhood was always supposed to be a joy. But then Monica was so *impossible*, many days it felt more like a wrestling match than a joyride. When my husband and I were considering another child, he actually said with fear, "But what if we have another Monica?" Even with our hesitation, we had two more children: Tim, sixteen months after Monica was born, and Joseph, six years after Tim was born. The boys were tough too, but Monica definitely took the award for most challenging child.

Why does it seem like others float through parenting like Mary Poppins, gliding in and out on an umbrella? *Why can't I be like Mary Poppins?* As an infant, Monica would bang her head on the mattress in her crib, leaving red marks across her forehead. Mary Poppins never had to deal with that! I'd wonder, *How am I supposed to raise her if she is pushing me around?*

Being a mom can be tougher than you ever imagined, and we need to know where we are going and what our end goal is. Parenting is a marathon. If we don't have focus along the way, we can veer off course, especially on days where peace seems to be a distant island. Even a trip to the bathroom includes banging on the door and screams of "Mommy! What are you doing?!" You're in there just long enough to have artwork drawn on hallway walls with permanent red marker. (I'm not the only one who had red marks down walls, am I?)

A target can get you through. This was mine.

> *My Life's Mission Statement:*
>
> To strive to love and know God more each day, to glorify God in all that I do, and to be a conduit of His love to others.
>
> To be a helpmate to my husband and help make him all that God wants him to be by being a constant support and encouragement for him.
>
> To raise children who love and follow God.
>
> To guide, support, and encourage them to be all that God intended them to be, striving for their very best in all they do.

If I were to edit this, today it would say "striving for good enough" instead of "their very best." All my kids tend to be a bit perfectionistic. (So, like I stated earlier—*Get some therapy.*) And I think I would also add "and help them fail as often as possible." In addition—even though my adult kids all love God today, that is a choice each person makes. Just as God gives us grace to choose, we parents can lead our kids to Jesus Christ, but it is their choice. We can't save our kids, only God can. We are all saved by grace—not by the guiding of our parents. Don't put that on yourself. Again, grace.

This mission statement was the best I could do at the time. You can do better. I signed it, and it hung on the side of our refrigerator. You may think it's silly, but it kept me focused on my end goal for each of my children. Little boys turn into men; little girls turn into women. Then they leave.

The Bible says in Proverbs 14:1, "The wise woman builds her house, but the foolish tears it down with her own hands." Have you ever noticed the next verse? Proverbs 14:2 begins with "One who walks in his uprightness fears the LORD." If we are to have balance and focus, we need to keep our eyes on God. Start each day with an awareness of God's presence and a prayer of thanks. Make God the center of your home and the center of each day. Life moves so fast that we sometimes don't take the time to stop and listen to God's voice.

I recently watched a video of Joshua Bell, one of the foremost violinists to ever live. As an experiment, he went to the metro station in Washington, D.C., and played for thousands passing by. *Only one* woman stopped to listen. Men, women, and children briskly walked past, underappreciating the beautiful talent. Don't allow the cares of this world to swallow you up so you miss the beautiful things God has placed around you. And especially don't be too busy or distracted that you can't hear God's voice. As you learn to listen well, you will become a better parent.

Keep your eyes on the finish line and on the Lord. A continual awareness of the end goal will renew your commitment for parenting with focus. As you peer into your little boy's eyes, remember that one day he will be a man—a man who will make decisions and choices completely apart from you. Some you will agree with and some not. As you hold your baby girl, remember one day she will pack up her stuff and move out of your house.

We do not raise kids; we raise adults. One day in the not-so-distant future, the house will be quiet; the kitchen will be spotless; you'll have plenty of time in the shower; and you'll be waiting by the phone, hoping one of your children will call or, even better, come for a visit. It seems like a long way off, but that day will come sooner than you think. The season of parenting little ones is short in the scope of your life—in the scope of eternity. But the effects of those few short years will have lifelong, generational, and eternal consequences. If you think of it like a timeline, the years on your child's timeline are mostly adult years. You are raising an adult.

THE BALANCING ACT

Being a mom is an everyday balancing act—it's like being the person in the circus who does everything. You balance the plates, juggle the balls, walk the tightrope, and swallow the swords. Maybe you are making the impossible happen. If you are a working mom, you are balancing plates. If you are in a marriage that is crumbling and you are staying the course, you are juggling balls and walking a tightrope. If your child is extremely strong-spirited and difficult, you are swallowing swords. If you are a single parent, you are walking a tightrope and swallowing swords. You are making the impossible happen.

The requests keep rolling in, and the nice lady from church keeps calling you to help with the children's class, while the dog keeps throwing up on your new carpet. No matter how tired you are, your husband still thinks you need a roll between the sheets at the end of the day, but you can think of nothing but sleep.

It is a balancing act, one that needs learning—fast. Without balance, you will be pulled in multiple directions and feeling like you live on that slip-and-slide in your backyard. With God's help, you can find balance.

It's all about priorities. When we are clear about what is most important to us, it's easier to adjust our day accordingly. That's where a mission statement comes in. Being mindful of the reality that children leave and husbands stay will help put things in perspective. When they see you loving God and your husband, you're giving them a model to follow.

As you make decisions, take a beat and ask yourself, "Is this best for my family?" and "Is this best for *me*?" Balance your life in such a way that, as you make decisions, your family comes out on top, making sure you have the capacity to do all the things you are saying yes to. And who knows, maybe then you'll be up for a little fun with your husband at the end of the day or have time for a nice long bath. If you need to cut something out, don't make it your family. And don't make it you. Please take care of you. To care for others, taking care of you will be key. We will talk more about this in chapter 5. Also, seek out other moms who can give you good, sound biblical guidance and understanding. Sometimes just to have someone say, "Yes, I totally understand! My kid does that too!" can make all the difference in the world.

SISTER, I'M CHEERING FOR YOU

Every mom deserves cheers at the end of each day; I hope you will feel cheers jumping from these pages. My prayer is that this book will inspire you to accept yourself and to learn, grow, and fully embrace and love your child-rearing years. Please know every page has been prayed over, and I've prayed for *you*. The years of raising my kids have ended, but now I can pass on what God taught me.

To my daughter I'd like to say, "Sweetheart, you look so pretty, and I'm so proud of you." It's never too late to right our wrongs.

You will hear from my daughter at the close of each chapter to give you a richer, more colorful understanding. This is where this book is different: you will get a view into the mind of an *impossible kid* and hear her thoughts, critiques, and perspective as a child—and as a mother. And please know that she is writing whatever she chooses to write. She received carte blanche to be honest and real, giving you uncensored feedback.

I'm thrilled you are taking this journey with us. Welcome, Mom. Hold on tight. These years will be over in a flash.

— — — — — — — — — — — — — —

THOUGHTS FROM MONICA:

"What if we get another Monica?"

Growing up, this statement was quite funny to me. It

became my badge of honor as a teenager. Goodness, how incredibly strong-willed does a child have to be for any parent to say this? I caused so much trouble, and I did it with style.

But now as a parent with two children, I must admit that child number two almost didn't happen. When I had to convince my husband I wanted to have a second baby, my husband fearfully looked into my eyes and asked, "But what if we end up with another Jake?" That's right, folks, God has a great sense of humor. I ended up with an impossible little boy. There have been two times in my life when I appreciated my mother more than anything. First was when I got married and moved out of her home. The second? That was when I had my firstborn. Nothing makes you appreciate your parents more than when you have children and realize they didn't quite deserve all the harsh criticism you threw their way.

As an adult, it's interesting to look back at what my mother experienced as a wife and mom. I can empathize and cry with her in the fear of bringing your first newborn home. And I can more than identify with her in the struggle of raising me. But when I was a child, she was a rock. She was infallible. I saw her as strong, beautiful, and self-assured. I thought nothing I said and did affected her, which was why I genuinely tried to go after her. I wanted to see how much I could poke the lion before I ticked it off. But my mother wasn't the clawing or roaring type—that was more my shtick.

I also find it interesting to see how the perspective of my parents, especially my mother, has significantly changed over the years. The older I get, the more complex of a woman she becomes to me—the richer a person I see. It makes me realize I shouldn't be so harsh on myself when I feel like I'm failing as a parent. It makes me realize that better parenting comes from a better marriage. And reading over her words, it makes me realize I need to stay rooted in my faith and be in earnest seeking of the Lord. How do I know this? Well, therapy sure has been helpful. But I know this because it's what Mom did. It's the example I was given. It's in the advice I receive from her.

And as amazing as my mom is, I must comment on that first day of high school...and that oh-so infamous red top. When I sat down, the sides of my shirt came up to show...*deep breath* ...a teeny tiny bit of side skin (*gasp*). I know, I know, truly indecent...or at least that's what Mom thought. I mean, I could understand her concern if maybe there was a thong sticking out or if you could see protruding hip bones. Nope, it was just a little squishy on the side.

Now, as an adult, this story makes the two of us laugh. It's hysterical. We both now know her response was disproportionate to my little amount of skin. We worked it out. We worked it through. I see now that her response came from a place of love and fear. It's a response I understand now that I'm a parent. I've already had to do my share of apologizing, and my kids are still very little. It happens in parenting. You're just not perfect. Sometimes, fear speaks before love. But above all, we need to have grace. And yes, at the time it did really hurt my feelings. But it didn't take away from the fact that my mom drove me to high school every day. And it didn't take away from the fact that she was always present. She wasn't perfect, but she always showed up and did her best. And I can only hope to do the same with my kids.

Allow me to leave you with some humor and hope. When my son was around eighteen months old, his strong nature and aggressive personality were already beginning to show. After doing something he wasn't supposed to, I placed him in his crib for a time-out. He spent his time-out screaming. He was ticked. But suddenly the screaming stopped, so I opened the baby camera app on my phone to see what was up. And what did I discover? Well, my son had ripped off his diaper and was proceeding to pee on his bed, on the crib bars, and he'd even decided to share the yellow fun with the wall.

So, let's all remember that I was the little baby who was banging her head on the crib mattress because she was ticked. Let's also point out that I'm a fully-functioning adult who no longer bangs her head on her bed. And at three years old, my son has ceased to pee on his bed when he's angry at me. Wherever your parenting journey is at, there is hope for us all that your child will make it to adulthood and be just fine.

— — — — — — — — — — — — — —

Thoughts to Ponder:

- Is it time to reevaluate your schedule?

- Are you tackling the job of parenting as you would a job you were getting paid for?

- Write a *Life's Mission Statement* and place it somewhere you look every day.

Chapter Two

KIDS LEAVE. HUSBANDS STAY.

A solid marriage is what I wanted to model for my kids. Mine needed work and an extra dose of TLC.

It was the middle of the night. My husband and I were arguing—and it was quite ugly. Our now-adult children were somewhere between five and seven years old at the time. They were just little darlings—innocent, impressionable, vulnerable. I wish I could say our yelling at each other at 2:00 a.m. was uncommon, but sadly it wasn't. We took the verse in Ephesians 4 about not letting the sun go down on your anger a bit too literally.

We were fueling the anger and not putting it to rest. And the kids? They had been awakened by another midnight matinee featuring screaming and door slamming. On this particular night, it was one of our worst. Nasty words were flying like hawks zooming in for the kill. We both had pretty much lost any sense of reason and had completely lost our minds. Control? *Pfft*. What's that?

What Mike did next exemplifies how crazed we both were. He went into the kids' room—for a talk. I heard him say, "Mom and I are getting a divorce. . .who would you like to live with?" He was calm. Like a raving-mad lunatic, I ran to the room. Poking my head in, I screamed, "Don't listen to him! We are NOT getting a divorce! Dad is just mad at me. GO BACK TO SLEEP!" Then I pointed at him and demanded, "YOU knock it off!"

"Kids, go back to sleep!"

It's a family joke now. Even our youngest, who wasn't born at the time, has heard the story of "the night Dad said they were getting a divorce and Mom came storming in yelling like a crazy person." We all laugh about it now, but at the time it wasn't funny at all. It was sad. Really sad.

Here's today's happy news: our marriage is strong, where nights are full of cuddles, security, and connection. Even so, due to the fights my children witnessed, regrettably, I'm sure they have many discussion topics for therapy. Should we have kept it from them? Well, we tried as much as possible, but when you're loud and slamming doors, it's a little too late.

HANDLING THE FALLOUT FROM FIGHTS

When there are disagreements in front of the kids or behind doors and the kids know it, hear it, and/or feel the tension from it, how do we handle this with them?

Sadly, sometimes kids think conflict between parents is somehow their fault, and they internalize it. Do we suck it up and never have conflict in front of the kids? If that were even possible, I don't believe that's the best for our kids. Refusing to communicate, nonverbal anger, and withdrawal can be worse, having long-term effects on our children. Open communication, on the other hand, can be helpful for their emotional health. When they see adults resolve conflict, it can instill better coping skills and emotional security in them. Seeing you make up and especially seeing hugs and kisses can give them a feeling of safety with a resolve that everything is okay.

Let your kids know even happy couples have disagreements, that it's normal to feel angry. But keep in mind if we are yelling in front of our kids, it tells them that yelling is the "grown-up" way to handle anger. This can be a fine line. We want to model anger in a healthy way, but we don't want our kids to think yelling is the way to resolve conflict. Working through all of this may require professional therapy.

As for me, I minimized how much our conflict affected our kids because I had a difficult time dealing with my own feelings let alone dealing with my kids' feelings. If I could go back, I would help my kids process and better handle the feelings *they* had during family conflict and give them a safe place to talk about their emotions. What we did do was either allowed our kids to watch how we resolved things or talked with them later and explained we worked it through, that we loved them and each other, and that Mom and Dad were okay.

HANDLING CONFLICT BETTER

How we handle conflict affects everyone around us. Anyone in my family will tell you that I'm a supreme fighter. Any argument I had "won" was a huge loss to our relationship. I had to learn to be a humble listener. Filtering everything through the truth that *my husband loves me and would not want to hurt me; we are on the same team* has been a huge help.

Conflict usually arises because of hurt or misunderstood feelings, and listening is key to resolution. The next time you have a disagreement with your spouse, sit back and try to understand from their perspective.

Ask yourself:

- Is there any validity to what's being said?
- What's my responsibility here?
- What do I need to learn from this situation?
- Do I owe them an apology?

If you can recognize the other's point and say, "You're right, I'm sorry," it will usually end the argument. When my husband does this, it stops me in my "I-don't-like-you-right-now" tracks. If you can keep calm and reasonable, you'll make better headway to happily ever after.

As you listen, you may discover their irritation has nothing to do with you. It's possible they are merely reacting to something from their past. The more we listen, the more we find out who they are. When it's your turn to talk, talk with a goal of resolution not an attempt to "win." Winning is losing in the couple fighting world.

Using "I feel" will get you much closer to oneness instead of "You did." The word *you* tends to put the other on the defensive. We all know this, but it can be so hard to do, which is why we continually need to be in process and working on ourselves.

Conflict actually has the potential to draw a relationship closer if it's handled well.

When it seems like a resolution isn't in sight, set up another agreed upon time to revisit the subject. Ephesians 4:26 says, "BE ANGRY, AND YET DO NOT SIN; do not let the sun go down on your anger." So, this means you stay up all night and fight it out, right? No. Table it and go to bed. It's amazing what rest and sleep can do for a conflict. My husband and I have done this, and oftentimes we are laughing in the morning at our pettiness the night before.

Some days you just do the best you can, and that must be good enough. If you are self-aware and can see your own weaknesses, you are above the curve. It took work and time to get to a better place in our marriage. One of the best gifts you can give your children is a home where Mom and Dad love each other and have a strong marriage—fights and all.

MARRIAGE IS A FAMILY AFFAIR

Marriage takes work. Investing in your marriage is investing in your children. Being centered on your marriage and not on your children will give your kids a healthier family environment.

As you've already figured out, Mike and I didn't have a good start in our marriage. We both entered with a lot of baggage, and we've been unpacking ever since. Our communication now? Way better than it was and getting better and better. Because we work at it. This didn't come easy.

I had come from a long line of heavyweight female leaders. My mother still has one central belief: the oldest living female is the boss of the family. Growing up, my mother always dressed my father—and still does. I've heard this type of interaction many times: my dad yelling from the bedroom, "Honey, what am I wearing today?" My mother yelling from the kitchen, "I'll be there in a minute to pick it out." In the meantime, Dad throws something on. Then Mom's in the bedroom saying, "No, you can't wear that. It's too small." Dad says, "But I want to wear this." Mom says, "No! It makes your stomach look big. Take it off!" Dad concedes, "Okay, then what can I wear?"

It's really kind of cute. They seem to like it this way, so who am I to criticize? Then there was my grandmother, Millie, my mother's mom, a lovable big Italian woman who yelled at my grandfather regularly. Grandpa asked, "Millie, where's my shirt?" Her reply, "On the back of the door, stupid!"

She also sent him on errands. She'd be demanding, "Andy, go down to Barone's and get me some bread and pepperoni, and then stop at Carmen's and pick up some cake!" My grandfather didn't drive, so he walked and he didn't complain. Ever! However, often by the end of the night, you could find Grandpa across the street at Spirito's Restaurant. . .at the bar.

My grandparents were wonderful, and I loved them dearly. They deeply loved each other and all us kids; that's just how they were, and we were used to it. I never really gave it much thought. Until I was married.

I didn't grow up with any kind of faith in our home. If we talked about God, it was usually as a joke. Dad, who was and still is an atheist, would say regarding church, "I'm going to Saint Mattress." Mom was a Catholic who rarely went to church, and if my family owned a Bible, I had no idea where it was. They were "expressive." The volume was high, and conflict was abundant. My parents did the best they could, and I knew they loved me and each other, but how does one change patterns you don't want for your family? How do you change the course of a colossal and generational ship?

Marriage brings out our rough edges—edges we need to deal with. I had multiple gotta-deal-with edges. Almost always, the beginning of any positive change in marriage is a good hard look at yourself. I knew I had a lot of work ahead of me, and I knew the work would never be done.

I needed to put my best efforts into my marriage to give my children a firm foundation. Bottom line, I had a lot of changing to do. How about you? Does your marriage need some tweaking? Do you need to hand over the reins to God and let Him guide you with your marriage and parenting?

Spending time with God daily would be my foundation for changing the course of my family. Perhaps *wrestling* with God would be more accurate. Shortly after making a commitment to follow Jesus Christ, my friend Dawn explained submissiveness to me. Wanting to argue with her, I was thinking, "What? I have been fighting for five years to get the ground I have, there is NO WAY I am giving it up now!" Then she showed me scriptures:

> *Wives, subject yourselves to your*
> *own husbands, as to the Lord.*
> EPHESIANS 5:22

> *It is better to live on a corner of the roof,*
> *than in a house shared with a contentious woman.*
> PROVERBS 25:24

She had me at contentious woman. I thought marriage was about fighting for control and holding your position like a war game. I was certainly not going to wave any white flag; no self-respecting woman did that. I hated it. I was angry.

My reply to God: "No way!"

Then it was as if God said to me, "Do you trust Me? You will not have to do this alone. I'll be with you completely along the way."

My desire was to have a relationship overflowing with love, fun, spunk, respect, and romance. Who doesn't want that, right? I asked God for a marriage that honored Him, then committed it to prayer and asked Him to help me.

An excellent wife, who can find her? For her worth
is far above jewels. The heart of her husband trusts
in her, and he will have no lack of gain. She does
him good and not evil all the days of her life.
PROVERBS 31:10–12

"Lord, is it possible I could be this kind of wife?" I was doubtful but had hope. When you decide to follow Jesus Christ, you need to give Him access to *everything*, even your marriage. As you trust God with everything and sit at His feet and allow Him to pour in, you will grow in ways you never thought possible. I truly believe one way you can see a woman's heart for the Lord is by how she treats her husband …even an ex-husband. Children are impacted greatly by the adult relationships surrounding them.

Before we move on, let's have a chat about submissiveness. Ephesians 5:21 says, "And subject yourselves to one another in the fear of Christ." One another. This goes both ways. So, what are we to do with this? In a marriage that honors God, both parties are looking out for the other and yielding for what is best for the relationship. Sometimes this means taking better care of yourself—we need balance. Sometimes it means yielding. I don't like the word *submissiveness*. I prefer to define it as a willingness to yield out of love and respect for the other person. Above all, choose love (1 Peter 4:8).

What if you don't have a husband like this? All we can do is start with ourselves and pray God works in our marriage. Take care of our side of the street, and give God the rest. Invite God to be part of your marriage. In doing so, recognize only God can meet all our needs; we can't look to another nor can we be that for another. You are a completely separate and whole person on your own and in a marriage where you get to choose who you will be—knowing you only have control over you.

What we believe about ourselves and about our marriage will shape our reality. Proverbs 23:7 says, "For as he thinks within himself, so he is." If we believe it's up to our husband to make us complete or to bring happiness or to make us whole or to be responsible for our needs, then we are placing overwhelming expectations on another person. Anytime we feel unloved, we might be tempted to blame our spouse for whatever we feel we're lacking. We need to be okay all on our own, a beautiful and lovable person, a whole complete person who chooses to be connected to another. One who offers love and intimacy and welcomes love and intimacy.

WE REAP WHAT WE SOW

The husband-and-wife relationship sets the pace and temperature of the home. "In sickness and in health" and *let not the kids pull us apart*. And remember—kids leave; husbands stay. I needed to figure out how to make my husband a priority and not have a kid-centered home. My natural tendency was to focus on my kids. It was certainly easier too, but *he* was there, so I had to figure this husband thing out.

Genesis 2:24 says, "For this reason a man shall leave his father and his mother, and be joined to his wife; and they shall become one flesh." Hey, wait, shouldn't it say Mom, Dad, *and* children all become one flesh? That's how I wanted it to read. Oh please, how does a "good" mom put her husband above her children? He's a full-grown capable man; he can fend for himself.

Unfortunately, this type of thinking doesn't prepare our children to leave and become their own separate selves—separate from us. Most likely, they will be gone from our home longer than they live in our home. What do we want to send them off with?

An intimacy void between husband and wife creates a frightening gap and puts a home off balance. We are made for connectedness, and when there's a vacuum in the marital relationship, the tendency might be to fill it with our children. And it's so easy to fill the void with our children. However, in the long run, this will hurt our children. It's imperative that we build into our marriage and have a life outside our kids. I found myself having to regroup and refocus from time to time.

Giving attention to my marriage helped me stay balanced.

I recall pondering how simple it seemed when my husband was out of town and I could focus entirely on my kids. I often felt pulled in so many directions, and it seemed impossible to be a good and attentive mom and still be a wife he wanted to come home to. Easy is not always best. Kids seeing Mom and Dad loving and caring for each other will pay off in benefits beyond the time they live in your home. One of my greatest joys is watching my children loving their spouses and modeling a marriage relationship for their kids.

As you focus on your marriage and "do nothing from selfishness or empty conceit, but with humility consider one another as more important than yourselves" (Philippians 2:3), you will gain more than you imagined and your children even more so.

Galatians 6:7 says, "Do not be deceived, God is not mocked; for whatever a person sows, this he will also reap." As this applies to all aspects of our lives, it definitely applies in our marriages. The more I followed God's principles, the better my marriage got. "No way," became, "yes way," when God had the reins.

Ephesians 5:33 says, "Nevertheless, as for you individually, each husband is to love his own wife the same as himself, and the wife must see to it that she respects her husband." I like to think of respect for my husband like the gas gauge in my car. If it's low and unaddressed, I could find myself not liking my husband and stuck on the side of the loveless road. We can always find fault with our mates, *and* we can always find things we adore and respect about them too. Does he work hard? Is he good with the kids? Does he empty the dishwasher or take care of the cars? Look for good, ponder the good, and bring up the respect meter. We get to choose what we think on. We can pick on him and find fault, but that's not good relationship making. Or good love making.

> *"I am my beloved's, and his desire is for me."*
> SONG OF SOLOMON 7:10

> *"His mouth is full of sweetness. And he is*
> *wholly desirable. This is my beloved and this*
> *is my friend, you daughters of Jerusalem."*
> SONG OF SOLOMON 5:16

Is he still your hunka hunka burning love? If not, how can you get back there? It usually starts with a mind-set. If we are allowing our minds to think about negative traits or perceived negative actions, "getting close" becomes "don't even think about it, buddy." On the contrary, turning those destructive thoughts into thanksgiving and gratefulness can transform our marriage and desire. What we focus on throughout the day will have huge ramifications in the love department. When a negative thought begins, turn it around. Turn "I hate it when he leaves his socks in the middle of the living room" to "Thank You, God, for a man with big feet." Then you can either leave the socks there as a reminder of why you love your husband or pick them up and be grateful for a man to share your life with. After a while, seeing the socks will bring feelings of endearment instead of irritation.

Let's say you had a friend who was incessantly bugging you about your socks or your [you fill in the blank]. How long would you remain her friend? Would you avoid this person? Would you want to sit and talk with her? When we have friends who stop being nice to us, we tend to find new friends. And yet, in our marital relationships, we don't give this much thought.

Sometimes in marriage people feel "stuck with the other person." I say, don't be stuck, be lovestruck. Remember when you were his girlfriend? A girlfriend flirts, doesn't criticize, laughs at his jokes, looks her best, compliments him, will go anywhere just to be with him, and typically adores her man. In a nutshell, she is very conscious of loving the man of her dreams and will do anything within reason to win her prize. Every day, remind yourself that he is your beloved and a gift from God.

WHAT ABOUT ME?

Being a stay-at-home wife and mother was hard for me to reconcile. Is this it? *Lord, I have many aspirations and big dreams—is this really what I am supposed to do—stay home?* Over the years, I was able to use my gifts and talents in numerous ways. God has a way of doing that if we offer Him our all: "The mind of a person plans his way, but the LORD directs his steps" (Proverbs 16:9).

I was listening to an interview with former first lady Michelle Obama, during which she talked about this very subject and how she gave up her career as a lawyer. She said, "The thing that really changed it was the birth of our children. I wasn't really ready for that; that really made it harder; something had to give, and it was my aspirations and dreams. I made that concession not because he [her husband] said you have to quit your job, but it felt like, I can't do all of this, so

I have to tone down my aspirations. I have to dial it back."*

Dialing it back is a good way to put it. We all need to make the decisions that are best for our family. It looks different for all of us—for some it's taking the job, and for others it's quitting a job. I saw greatness and leadership in my husband, I believed in our family, and I believed God would use my decision for good. And He did. God later turned my husband into a pastor, a pastor who understands struggle in relationships and has helped countless families and marriages.

As you raise your kids, you are influencing the world. A mom who teaches her children to love others is changing the world for good. It doesn't matter what profession you choose; if you exemplify love, kindness, and acceptance, you are an example of Jesus Christ. We don't know what the future holds, but we can trust God with our future—He "directs our steps."

When I became an author, that was truly beyond all my wildest dreams. Me? Someone who had trouble reading as a kid, panicked when asked to read out loud, and used CliffsNotes through high school? God takes all our shattered dreams, failed attempts, and injured souls, and He gives us a place to shine. He takes what's broken and battered and makes it beautiful.

For more marriage resources, check out my other books, *From Me to We* and *The Intimacy You Crave*. God has a way of using our struggles to help others. Embracing and accepting who we are paves the way for us to give and receive love.

*Netflix, *Becoming* (May 6, 2020)

ACCEPTANCE

We all long for acceptance and love. I want to be accepted for who I am. All of me. All my faults. Failures. Mistakes. I long for complete acceptance. Don't you? We need to offer what we long for ourselves.

One of the best gifts we can give our spouse is full acceptance—for all his rough edges and stuff that bugs us. Can we embrace him fully just as he is? If "stuff" is driving us crazy, this says more about us than it does about him. That's when it's time to look inward. Ask, "Why does this bug me so much?" Like marriage and family therapist Jim Beebe instructs, "My husband is not my problem. He can be a problem, but he's not *my* problem. I am my problem." And, "No matter what I do, I am totally responsible for what I think, feel, say, and do."

Romans 15:7 tells us, "Therefore, accept one another, just as Christ also accepted us, for the glory of God." This truth exemplified in our families is powerful.

My goal was to teach my kids the love of God—His perfect love and acceptance—then offer my kids my human and flawed love and acceptance. Now that we've landed on flawed, let's circle back to the fallout from marital disagreements.

GIVE GOD YOUR MISTAKES

Over the years, I have made many mistakes in my marriage. God was always there to pick me up and direct me in the right way. Several times when I felt destroyed, distraught, and hopeless, I'd turn to my Bible, and the answer was staring me in the face. When I blow it with my husband, I ask for forgiveness, and then I get to start over. Being able to use the words *I'm sorry, please forgive me* and *I'll work on this* are so freeing. I feel like those words are my redeeming words.

Whatever your mistakes or if you have a difficult situation or have fights during zero-dark hundred, God can fix it and turn it into something beautiful that honors Him. Just do the best you can. That's what I did.

> *For the LORD God is a sun and shield; the LORD*
> *gives grace and glory; He withholds no good*
> *thing from those who walk with integrity.*
> PSALM 84:11

— — — — — — — — — — — —

THOUGHTS FROM MONICA:

I asked a counselor once, "How can I become a better parent?" His response was "Be marriage-centered and not child-centered—have a good marriage." And that point, boy, did it really stick with me. I certainly don't have this parenting thing figured out, because I'm nowhere near an expert on marriage. Might as well give up, right? The whole family's doomed 'cause Mommy's got issues. Let's think this through. I want to be a good mother, so be a good wife. I want to be a good wife, so be a good person. How do I become a God-fearing, husband-loving supermom? I work on my issues.

I remember my mother telling me, "Monica, the issues you have with us in our home, those issues are going to carry into your own marriage. They're not going to magically go away because you're in love. Work on it now."

Well, Mom, I'd love to publicly tell you, "You were wrong," but nope. You were entirely right. As you have already intuited, I put up a fight as a child, and I've carried that same fight into my marriage. My husband has had to say to me many times that he's not the enemy, we're on the same team. And he's right. I've had to learn how to strip away my coping strategies and talk about my feelings so hubby and I can reach resolution.

This was one thing I always saw and always experienced with my parents: resolution. Every fight and every conflict were dealt with. Mom and Dad didn't just explode and then ignore it ever happened. They resolved it between them and then resolved it with us. It didn't look perfect, but fights ended with a period. Thankfully, I'm married to a man who works toward resolution with me. We end our conflicts with peace and resolve. And if an argument was started in front of the kids, we go to them and let them know that Mommy and Daddy are fine, everything is okay, and it is not their fault.

As our son has aged and become more aware of our arguments, it has taken me back to that scared little girl watching my parents argue. In my youngest years, I remember many arguments between Mom and Dad. (I think it might be the plight of an eldest sibling because my second-oldest brother doesn't remember the fighting as much.) Every time they were in a verbal brawl, I was held captive and I obsessed over it. Every time they fought, I would get a rock in the pit of my stomach, mixed with nerves and butterflies. I would feel sick. Sometimes I cried. And then if they were in a room arguing with the door closed, I would perch myself at the foot of the door listening as the anxiety grew within me. Each fight felt as if it would end in their divorce—that was my greatest fear.

It slowly became clear through the years that Mom and Dad were always going to work it out. As my parents matured in Christ and as people, the arguments became less and less and less intense. And as I grew up and developed a sense of autonomy, their fights ceased to bother me. Mom and Dad worked it out, and they worked to put the family back in peace. My husband and I have carried on this same style. He and I may talk about our own feelings from a fight, but we've realized we need to give our children words for *their feelings* when we fight. As my mom mentioned prior, she didn't have the tools to help us process our feelings when it came to their arguments. And I look back at that now, and all I have to say is it's okay.

It's so very fine. No parent can give their child everything. I can only give and teach my children what is already in my toolbox. I cannot give them things I do not have. My point: now as a parent myself, I can't help but feel grace for my mom. This parenting thing is HARD. And the only way I'm going to become a better parent is to work on my own issues, because that work filters through my marriage and lands on my kids. At the end of the day, you do the best you can with what you've been given, and then you give the rest to God.

— — — — — — — — — — — — —

Thoughts to Ponder:

- Have you been placing your children above your husband? If so, is it time to reevaluate your priorities?

- Have you been showing honor and respect to your children's father? Between you and God, ask God to help you with this.

- Are you content with the communication level in your family? What steps do you need to take and what changes need to be made in order to have better communication in your family?

Chapter Three

THE PARENTING MYTH

As long as I do everything right, then my kids will turn out okay.
That was my unspoken and subliminal internal belief.

Monica was just weeks old, and my mother (who was visiting) and I were frantically trying to figure out what was wrong because she wouldn't stop crying. No matter what we did—hold her, rock her, feed her, change her diaper—we couldn't calm her down. We decided we better take her temperature; something must be wrong.

Rectal thermometers were the only way to go back then, and we had to hold her down while she screamed. After a long, agonizing three minutes, the thermometer read 102.7. We both freaked! As we panicked, one of us screamed, "Call the doctor!"

With a pounding heart and shaky voice, I explained to our pediatrician's nurse that there was something terribly wrong with my baby. Just then, my husband calmly strolled in the room with thermometer in hand and asked, "Did either of you remember to shake down the thermometer to zero before you took her temperature?"

My next words were "I'm sorry, everything is fine."

My brave "knight-in-thermometer-armor" saved the day.

Would I ever get this mom thing right? There were daily reminders of how I was falling short.

Monica's fits didn't help my mom self-esteem. I was feeling like a failure much of the time and needed to reach out for help and advice. Monica "inspired" me to seek God, seek counsel, and devour parenting books and material. The Lord showed me a strong will was actually a good thing and a gift, as long as we learned to direct and train her carefully and in a way that didn't break her spirit. We've all heard it said, "A doctor is practicing medicine." So why can't we just say, "We are practicing parenting"? Because that's what it felt like to me—practicing.

Firstborn children seem to get the largest portion of our "practicing." And regrettably, Monica had to witness more of our rocky years in marriage than her brothers had to endure. After hearing us argue, she'd ask, "Mommy, are you and Daddy getting avorced?" *Bring on the guilt and self-loathing.* The fact that she couldn't even pronounce the word was a double gut punch.

"No, sweetheart, Mommy and Daddy are not getting divorced. We love each other very much." (Mommy and Daddy just act like morons sometimes and would rather sweep it all under the playpen, but now we must deal with it because you're asking about it.)

We would reassure her that Mommy and Daddy loved

each other, her, and God, and we'd work out whatever was needed. Honest conversations with our kids can be painfully uncomfortable but oh so critical. If she wanted to talk about it, we talked about it.

And this seems like a good time to say I had no idea, until I read it in the previous chapter, that she would sit at the foot of our door and listen in. Seriously, no clue. How could she have kept that from us for so many years? She was strong-willed and sneaky. So, check behind closed doors. I wish I had.

LEARNING AND GROWING

How many times have you been on a plane and seen a mom with a baby? I always make it a habit to smile at those brave moms. My daughter and son-in-law were preparing for a flight with their two little ones and asked me for input. What I said was: prepare for the worst—spit, vomit, poop, fits, crying—but focus on your own sanity and resolve. Your calm and fun demeanor will translate to the kids. Even if things don't go as well as hoped, you'll be okay.

Just like when the oxygen masks lower on an airplane, we need to put ours on first—taking care of you first will have big payoffs for your kids. In turn, we need to deal with and process our own feelings to help our children do the same. How can we help our kids if we ourselves don't embrace our feelings and pain? This was an area where I fell short.

When Monica would cry, I'd say, "Don't cry, honey, it'll be okay," or I'd try to help her fix whatever problem she was having. What I needed to do was acknowledge her pain and offer empathy and understanding without trying to "fix" her.

Why did I try to stop her from deeply feeling in this way? Because I myself couldn't deal with her pain and needed it to stop because it was too painful for *me*. It starts with us. If we are going to help our children process emotions, we need to process and embrace our own emotions. We can only give what we ourselves have, which is why we need to be committed to learning and growing.

Now when she cries, even though she is an adult, I don't try to stop her. I listen and offer compassion and understanding. She feels comfortable talking to me because coming to Mom is a safe space. This enriches our connection and relationship. It would have been a huge benefit to her if I could have done this in her younger years. As we learn and grow, we can help our children do the same.

Think of a six-year-old playing with friends and throwing a fit when playtime is over. A mom could say, "How dare you act like that" or "You should be grateful that you got to play with your friends," but that's not going to help your child process their anger. Instead, offer understanding by saying something like "I see that you're angry and sad because it's time to go home and you want to play more. It's okay to be mad, but it's not okay to throw a fit. You can sit here quietly until you are ready to talk about it."* If your child is anything like mine was, quiet and angry just don't go together, but we can ask for it and model self-control even when they are out of control.

Has your child ever thrown a fit in a grocery store while strangers look on with judgment? I heard about a mom having a difficult time packing her kids and her groceries in the car, and another mom walked over and asked, "Can I help you?"

The frazzled mom began to cry. Moms need help not judgment.

"Fits in the grocery story are so much fun," said no mother ever. In the moment, there's not much you can do if you're in line and your darling is pitching a fit. How it's handled will make all the difference. Say to yourself, *Look at me being so brave to tackle the grocery store with judgmental onlookers and a small child. I'm amazing.*

One time while in a checkout line with my two older kids, my then-five-year-old son started screaming, "This is not my mom!" (Yeah, I taught him to do that if he needed help.) Luckily, the store staff knew me well enough to know it was my son. I gave him that Mom Look and threatened [you can imagine], and he stopped. Kids love to make scenes in public places; Monica, on the other hand, not so much.

Therefore, many of my "public" stories will feature Monica's brothers because, frankly, she saved the hoopla for us at home. Everywhere I went I heard about what a lovely, exceptional little girl I had—while thinking they had me confused with someone else. Eventually, I took the compliments as God's little pats on the back, telling me, "Hang in there, Mom, there's hope yet."

Satan is always waiting for an opportunity to cause havoc and divide a family. First Peter 5:8 says, "Be of sober spirit, be on the alert. Your adversary, the devil, prowls around like a roaring lion, seeking someone to devour." Embrace the personality traits of your child, and team up with your husband to create a united front. Mike and I knew early on we'd have to stay unified, and we had regular meetings to do so.

And if one can overpower him who is
alone, two can resist him. A cord of three
strands is not quickly torn apart.
ECCLESIASTES 4:12

Be unified as husband and wife, and lean on God for direction and wisdom, trusting when He says in His Word, "I will instruct you and teach you in the way which you should go; I will advise you with My eye upon you" (Psalm 32:8). We do not always know what to do, but God does, and He is always there waiting for us to pray and ask. You are not alone.

PRACTICING PARENTING

We kept trying new approaches until something worked. At times it was hard to like Monica, and I would ask God to give me a heart for her with compassion. What kind of a mother doesn't like her child? What was wrong with me? I always loved her, but I felt defeated by the effort it took to guide her.

One day when picking Monica up from grammar school, she realized she had forgotten something and had to go back to her classroom. I told her to hurry because we had an appointment. When I saw her walking back slowly, I hollered at her to run, and she went even slower. When she got to the car, I asked her why she didn't run, and she replied, "I didn't want to!"

Consequently, when her dad got home, he instructed her to run in the backyard while he ran with her. Most kids would think running with Dad was fun but not her. She screamed in anguish while she ran.

Our strategy was to give choices and a free voice in allowing our kids to express themselves. I wanted to hear thoughts and opinions to foster a relationship of trust and mutual respect. From the time our kids were very young, we did our best to communicate what the boundaries were and the consequences for choosing not to follow directives. Children like and need clear guidelines. When our children understood they had decision power to choose to follow our directives and make good choices, it gave them the responsibility for themselves, with an understanding that their choices would dictate the consequences. Isn't that how life is?

During a church service while Pastor Andy Stanley was interviewing his father, Dr. Charles Stanley, he told a story about getting his first traffic ticket as a teenager. Scared and not sure how his father would react, he handed the ticket to his father, who handed it back to him. He said, "Turn the ticket over and follow the instructions." He didn't get mad, he affirmed Andy by saying, "You can handle this yourself," and let him deal with the consequences. *

Similarly, as we parented, we stopped and thought about what natural consequences would look like. Most of our rules had to do with keeping them safe and those around them safe. When we told a child to do something, we expected a response. We were careful what we asked Monica to do because we knew it would most likely be a fight. We were careful to pick the battles that we knew we'd follow through on. She even verbalized once while talking about something her friend's parents did, "If you and Dad did that to me, I'd make your life miserable." And we knew she meant it.

Even the simplest of tasks took so much effort, like teeth

brushing. I'd ask if she had brushed her teeth, and she would adamantly say yes, but when I checked, it was obvious she hadn't. Do you then make her brush her teeth or deal with the lying? Addressing both was exhausting. *Just brush your teeth already! I don't have the energy for this.*

By the time Monica turned ten, she'd kick the wall in her bedroom with chants of "I hate 'em, I hate 'em, I hate 'em!" and this continued until the age of fifteen. One time her father and I went in and joined her in chanting, "I hate 'em, I hate 'em, I hate 'em." We all laughed. We'd let her express herself, and then once she calmed down, we'd talk with her about how she was feeling.

As you guide your child, pay attention to what works. Does it cause her to shut down emotionally or shut off toward you? If so, that may not be the best approach. You want to use correction that opens their heart toward you and God. When a child realizes what they did was hurtful—either to themselves or to another—and they made a bad choice, you're getting somewhere.

Calm and clear directives work best, along with hugs and reassurance. It's hard for a child to follow the rules if the rules keep changing or if they do not know what the rules are. Let them know it's their choice—they can follow the rules, or they can break the rules and deal with the consequences. Along the way, reaffirm your love and praise good choices.

The worst process to fall into is threatening. Make sure the consequence is something you are going to follow through with; otherwise, you're teaching them to not take what you say seriously. From a young age, your child knows what you will and will not follow through on.

Monica would oppose us until she decided to comply, and there was no telling what she'd do when we weren't watching. We talked with her until *she* decided to comply. Once she understood and adopted it as her own choice, that was it, the battle was over. Until the next incident. And the process would start all over. It was almost as if she were testing us to see if we would give up on her, and she was measuring our love for her.

We saw in her this strong, stubborn, never-give-up, never quit-till-I-get-what-I-want personality, and it often came with a good dose of dirty looks. At times I didn't feel like a grown-up human but a scared little girl trying to play house with a kid who was pushing me around.

Finally, I had to come to terms with the reality that I was going to make mistakes and that I needed to be satisfied with doing the best I could. *Make the mistake, learn from it, and move on.* The more I focused on my mistakes, the more mistakes I seemed to make; but when I focused on my victories and loving and enjoying my children, I grew as a mother, more and more content as they grew into each new phase. Don't beat yourself up over perceived mistakes; make amends, learn, and move on. Practice, right?

REFRAMING STRUGGLE

No mom wants to see their child struggle—it's painful and disheartening. But what if struggle is exactly what they need in order to soar? My two older children struggled throughout their childhoods. While Monica and Tim were in middle school, a uniform was required. I recall commanding my daughter to pull down her rolled-up shorts while ordering my son to pull up his sagging pants. I'd squawk, "You up, you down!" Looking back, did it really matter that much if pants were pulled up or lowered a bit? Today I'm not sure, but at the time it seemed right to address it.

Our youngest son, on the other hand, was the easiest to raise—compliant, cheerful, well adjusted, and popular with his peers. He excelled in school, served at church, and began working on staff at church at age sixteen. As a young child, most correction consisted of getting his attention and asking for a changed behavior. He'd say, "Okay, Mommy," and that was it.

Moving forward, Monica and Tim forged through into adulthood with amazing resolve. Both graduated from college, which they paid for themselves, and started careers upon graduation. Do you have a child who is fighting you? It's that same tenacity that will propel them into huge successes.

Except for his grammar school years, Joseph didn't seem to struggle much until he turned eighteen, and then the avalanche hit. He had seemed to float through his childhood and then grappled as an adult. Monica and Tim launched early, and Joseph, well let's just say he's got huge potential for launching. However, if I had to pick the kid who would buy me a car or a house in the future, I'd put my chips on Joseph. In the meantime, we are supportive as he works through figuring it out. When you are visibly seeing your child's struggles, you can guide and support and help them overcome.

Struggle produces a strong kid. James 1:2–3 says, "Consider it all joy, my brothers and sisters, when you encounter various trials, knowing that the testing of your faith produces endurance." These verses apply to our kids as much as they do us. Anytime you see your child struggling, be there with love and support, and acknowledge God is working. Trust God with your child. Learn to enjoy the struggle and be okay in it and welcome it. Your kid struggling now leads to their future success.

If you have a child with a very strong spirit, don't be alarmed. Embrace it and be thankful, for it is that same strong nature that will enable him or her to stand up against peer pressure. It is that same strong temperament that will enable them to make wise decisions and make good choices. It is that same strong personality that will lead others and conquer obstacles that others only dream of. Embrace it, and be there to guide your child. Adopting a mind-set of a marathon and not a sprint will help you for the long nurturing haul. "Let's not become discouraged in doing good, for in due time we will reap, if we do not become weary" (Galatians 6:9).

DEALING WITH SELF-JUDGMENT

I had to fight against daily judgment of myself. Mistakes and weaknesses and fumbles are sometimes met with our own self-judgment and doubt. When we are continually judging ourselves as parents, it's like having an internal mom report card.

- Made chocolate chip cookies. A+

- Ate most of the cookies ourselves. D-

- Kid eats one cookie and says, "Thank you, Mommy. I'll save the rest for another day." A

- Kid freaks out from eating too many cookies and throws up. D+
- Kid eats all their vegetables. A+
- Kid asks for cookies, and we yell, "I'm on a diet, stop asking for cookies!" F- and a dose of self-loathing for eating all the cookies *and* yelling.

When Monica and her younger brother were in grammar school, I was called to the principal's office after school. Expecting a bad report about one of my children, I went in with a minor level of anxiety only to be overjoyed to find out that Tim had handled himself well when a child hit him in the classroom. As I walked proudly across the schoolyard, I couldn't have been more delighted. *You're such a good mom! Oh yeah, oh yeah! Go, Mom!* Then, before meeting up with my kids who were playing, I was stopped by a teacher letting me know Tim had been in the boys' bathroom throwing wet paper towels against the wall. *Go, Mom!* turned into *What? Worst mom ever!* I went from an A to an F in a matter of minutes.

Somehow, we calculate that our child's compliance and obedience equal good parenting. Bad behavior equals bad mom. I wanted a world where angel-like glee clubs sang me mom praises with kids who always behaved because their mom was just that wonderful. It was sometimes hard to embrace my humanness.

Have you ever been introduced to someone in this manner?

"This is my friend Gail; she's a prostitute."

"Well, hello, umm. . .how's business?"

I've never had that experience, have you?

And yet, in the Bible I read, "Rahab, the prostitute." When

the Israelite spies needed a place to stay, where did they take refuge? At the home of Rahab, the prostitute (Joshua 2). Not just Rahab but Rahab *the prostitute*. Why in the world would they choose "the prostitute's" home? We could have many theories. The fact is God chose to highlight "a prostitute." Being a prostitute was part of her identity, her title.

What's your title? Mom? Working mom? Wife? Are you defined by your career choice? Do you feel labeled by others? How have you chosen to label yourself? Swap it for *Human. Lovable. Child of the King of the Universe.* Throughout the Bible, I see God saying, *No matter what you've done or what has happened to you or what label you have or how unruly your children are—you are loved; you have value; you're okay; and it's okay to be human.*

The message to ourselves, however, can taunt us that we need to be a superhuman mom. Throughout the Bible, God's message to us declares, *It's okay to be human.*

EMBRACING HUMANNESS

"As long as I do everything right, then my kids will turn out okay." The problem with this is we are leaving out free choice. The same free choice God gives every single one of His creations. We do not have control over our children's choices. You can do everything just right, and still your child can choose to walk away from God or make what we deem really poor life choices. Thinking you somehow have control over your child's destiny is crazy-making and puts undue pressure on yourself. I know; I've been a part of crazy-making.

What I've learned to do is first recognize I can't. I can't

control what my kids say and do. Second, acknowledge God can. God, the Almighty King of heaven and earth, is working and will care for my kids better than I can. And third, I'm giving it all to Him. God can carry the load; I can't. This is peacemaking.

By the time Monica turned sixteen, I felt like we had made huge progress, and then the older boyfriend entered the picture—and it felt like we started over. We'll talk about this in chapter 10.

At seventeen, a beauty emerged, and to give you hope, I'd like to share an excerpt of a letter Monica wrote me while I was attending a weekend retreat.

> *I just wanted to let you know how much I love you. You are the coolest mom. You do so much and get so little back. I want to thank you for all that you do. I really want to let you know that I see all that you sacrifice for me, and I can't express enough how grateful I am that you do that. I can only long and wish to have such devotion as you when it comes to God and family. I wish to have, one day, the great love and fear that you have of God. Mom, you are an amazing woman, and I can only wish to be half the woman that you are. I tell you that nothing you do is in vain. I'm watching and learning from you, and I like what I see.*

When you feel like you're not getting through, you are. When you feel like she isn't seeing all you do, she is. When you feel like he isn't paying attention to what you're doing, he is. What you do is not in vain. Your child is taking it all in. Triumph is on the other side, and it's worth it.

— — — — — — — — — — — — —

THOUGHTS FROM MONICA:

As I was reading this chapter, I found myself blushing from embarrassment. I honestly forgot how tough I was. And that statement doesn't even sum it up fairly. Yes, I was a well-behaved, good-mannered child out of the home, so that left my stubbornness, aggression, and anger to spew out in the home. Reflecting on my childhood, I can still recall those feelings I had toward my parents. I remember always feeling so very angry. I wanted to do things my way. I wanted to do it at my own pace. And if you got in my way, I would decimate you. At a young age, getting mad made me feel strong. I could push people around to get what I wanted. And particularly with my mother, I somehow knew my aggressive nature was opposite of hers, so I was always pushing to see if I could get under her skin and win.

Anger was an easily accessible emotion for me, so I figured out how to use it. But as I've aged, I've realized anger has been my way of not feeling sad or hurt. If I'm powerful, then you can't stop or hinder me. When my mom came to me as an adult and apologized for telling me not to cry as a child, I didn't think it any big deal. But as that apology had time to take root, I realized I needed to make peace with my internal sensitivity and just feel okay with crying. Her being open about this freed me to be okay with being more sensitive than I wanted to admit.

I've also had to come to terms with my aggressive nature, especially when it comes to parenting my son. He's like me in temperament. Getting mad is easy for him. And I blamed myself for every tantrum and outburst—that somehow I had given him my nature. Sometimes I'll cry to my husband that my shortcomings as a person are making me a terrible mother. And Kyle will remind me of the day we brought Jake home. We could not console him. He was fed; he was changed; he was dressed comfortably; and yet nothing we did would stop all the angry cries. He was uncomfortable and mad about it. He popped out like this. He is naturally strong-willed, and this is a good thing. Just as my mom did with me, so I will do with him. We're going to channel and direct that will. And the benefit of us being alike is that I can now give him the tools to manage his feelings that I didn't have as a kid.

Firstborns do have it rough. Most of the parenting mistakes land on us. And most of my parenting mistakes land on Jake. With the second, they throw a tantrum, and you know exactly what to do. *Stand back, everyone, I'm a professional.* With the first, it's all new. They're the science experiment. *Well, that didn't work today, so let's try something new tomorrow.* How can I not forgive my parents for their parenting missteps? I'm in the exact same conundrum now! Life and God—those two just have a way of exacting poetic justice.

Here is where I am now (and to also echo my mother): I can't control my childrens' destiny or their actions or their feelings, nor should I. I can't stop their public fits or outbursts of rage. I can't make my children become Christians. Their choices, lives, and faith are all in their hands. I can train, teach, and model. But in particular, I can let them just be. It's okay for them to be who they are. And it is okay for me to be who I am. I accept my shortcomings as a mother. I accept who I am as a person, and then I try to do better.

— — — — — — — — — — — — —

Thoughts to Ponder:

- Are your children growing up in a peaceful home where they see the love of Jesus? Is it time to take steps to create a better home environment?

- Are your discipline methods working? Is it time to take a different approach? Is your discipline causing your children to retreat from you?

- Do your children have a clear understanding of what the rules are?

*Milan & Kay Yerkovich, *How We Love* (Colorado Springs: WaterBrook, 2013): 43, (paraphrased).

Life, Love & Legacy: A Conversation with Dr. Charles Stanley, North Point Community Church, Dec. 6 & 13, 2020.

Chapter Four

INTENTIONAL TIME

On a recent grocery store trip with my now-adult son, I said, "I'll grab the eggs. You get the milk." A little later, he found me not in the egg aisle but in the soap aisle. Later during checkout, realizing I had never gotten the eggs, he said, "How did you raise kids? How are we all still alive?" I wonder that too.

I'm also in awe over how emotionally intelligent my kids are, even after some of the nutty things I told them. For instance, the start of my sex talk with my daughter was "Okay, now before I tell you anything, I want you to know God says sex is only for marriage, and if you have sex outside of marriage, then you could die." Geez! If I were texting you, I'd add the hand to the head emoji. (Full story later.) This worked with my first two kids, but my third child questioned me to the point I had to rescind my statement. Maybe telling my boys that their penis would fall off went too far.

Little Joey turned his head like a hesitant puppy and questioned, "Wait, Mom, how would you die? Would my penis really fall off?"

Going where I didn't want to go: "Well, if you have sex with more than one person and get a disease, then. . ."

"But, Mom, what if both of you have never had sex before?"

He had me at "Wait, Mom."

How does a mom come back after that? Lord, help me. If you've done a few things that you feel silly about, welcome to the Mom Club. You're a messy human just like the rest of us.

And, of course, these are the stories our kids will tell over and over so we never forget our faux pas. Yes, these stick, but what also sticks is how our children felt around us.

GRANDMA LOVE

I learned so much from my grandmothers about unconditional love and acceptance and feeling like you mattered. My grandma Eva loved God and going to church, and if you asked her what her spiritual gift was, she'd say, "Baking." No one could jump in her kitchen because the jumping would ruin the cake she had in the oven—which everyone knew had been stirred only clockwise while in batter form. She was known for saying, "It's not that I forgot, it's just that I can't remember," and "Fight nice." She would also often ask, "What's your name?" when she was unable to retrieve it. One time she came home and said she "almost" got into an accident. Grandma had hit another car three times because "the light changed and the car wasn't moving." Before she passed from Alzheimer's disease, my uncle asked her if she knew who he was. Her reply: "Well, maybe if you came around more often, I'd know who you were."

When my aunts and uncles reminisce about Grandma, some of their fondest memories are when she'd wake one of her kids in the morning, let them know they wouldn't be going to school, and tagged on, "Don't tell your father." Her kids felt loved, valued, and cherished, knowing Mom enjoyed spending time with them.

Like my grandmother, I did this too—minus the "Don't tell your father." I'd clear my schedule, pull a kid out of school—if they didn't have anything pressing—and we'd spend the day together. This continued until college, and I believe it was a key relationship builder. Even during college, Monica, who was local, and I would often meet for lunch. I'd drive to meet Tim, who was hours away, usually weekly. And with Joe, I got on a plane and spent a week in his college town.

Make space in your schedule for your kids. Make it a non-negotiable calendar event, which sets a precedent of showing value and being worthy of your time. The most valuable thing anyone can give you is his or her time—time given sends a message of love and importance. Giving time says "You are valuable."

In kindergarten, she comes home talking about monkey bars and coloring and who wet their pants in class. By the time she's a teenager, this escalates to "the boy next to me was talking about having sex with his girlfriend, and the kid behind me was sniffing something up his nose." We need to take the time to listen and talk and just *be* with our kids—no matter what age.

When Monica was seven, she wanted to know what

homosexuality was, and I told her I thought she was too young for the answer. Well, she asked Grandma. My dear mom was flustered but answered by saying, "In the rear." Oh boy. Lesson learned. I better answer her questions.

LISTEN, LISTEN, LISTEN

An impossible kid needs time to talk and process how she's feeling. Impossible kids are the kids who will stand up when others back down, and they need a place to be heard and understood. Usually, these are the kids who have a great deal going on in their quick brains.

With Monica, communication was essential. It is crucial to give your children a time to express themselves with no judgment or correction, a time for them to talk and you listen.

When Monica was in grammar school, I started "chat time." Every day after school, we spent an hour talking while we had treats, coffee, and hot chocolate. Her brother would go to another room to play, and it was just girl time.

With boys, chat time over tea isn't so appealing, but throwing a ball or going for ice cream is. It's amazing what you'll hear when you make space to listen while kicking a ball or slurping a chocolate milkshake.

I'd also go in Monica's room, sit, and wait for her to talk, which didn't take long. Her dad did the same.

The following are conversations with my three kids all in the same day.

Joey, age nine, while alone with me at McDonalds, pointing to a sign, "That's the old Ronald McDonald. I wonder who Ronald McDonald is today. Edgar says bad words. Trevor tattles a lot. There are six smart kids in my class: Nathan, me, Brittany, Samantha, Trevor, and Daniela. Daniela, she doesn't speak that much English, but she's pretty smart. See the marks on the top of the soda lids? Why do they have them? Mom, when God destroys the earth, will He make a new one?"

Tim, age fifteen, sitting at the park with me during Monica's softball practice while Joey played, "A girl in one of my classes asked me today if masturbation was a sin." And, "I was walking to one of my classes today, and Amber asked if she could put her hands in my pocket. I told her no. Then she asked if she could just grab on to me. I told her no, and she told me I was being mean."

Monica, age seventeen, while driving home, "Sonya, the girl who plays short stop, well, she's kind of a lesbian. Oh, today in one of my classes, Tiana put a second piercing in both of Mia's ears with a needle. Mia is hiding it from her mom, because her mom told her she couldn't double pierce her ears."

It starts with Ronald McDonald, who's smart in class, rises to masturbation, peer interactions, sexual identity, and needles. Talk and listen, listen, listen.

Sometimes it was hard not to overreact. I might be freaking out inside, but I'd respond with, "Well, now, that's interesting. What do you think about that?" Develop a good poker face to keep hearing the scoop.

My husband and I were strategic about carving out one-on-one time with each child. Anytime Mike was going somewhere, he would usually ask, "Who's coming with me?" and then he'd often stop for a soda or something on the way home.

With each of my kids, I noticed what they enjoyed doing

and created one-on-one time to share together—getting coffee, a donut, a burger, or lunch at the park. Desiring time with your children and making "dates" communicates they are cherished. Your engagement translates to their feeling valued and treasured. Feeling wanted and enjoyed develops self-worth.

Sometimes I'd get discouraged by all the traffic around my kids' schools and how it could take thirty minutes for what should be ten, until my friend who lost her teenager to a tragic accident told me one of the things she missed most was driving with her daughter on the way to school in the morning. I realized driving my kids was a gift.

Can I get in your car "business" for a moment? When your child is in the car with you, what are you doing? Are you on your phone or listening to something that doesn't interest her? Car rides have unlimited opportunities. It was in the car when Monica and I found out Tim "officially" had a girlfriend and it was also where I heard which boys Monica liked. Turn car time into bonding time by engaging your child without an agenda.

BLINDSIDED

Balancing your family, especially when you have multiple children, can feel like you are spinning plates and throwing a few too. Sometimes, the child who gives you the least amount of trouble gets the least amount of time and energy. Even "easy" children need our time and attention, and when you have an impossible child challenging you at every turn, you can lose track of your other children.

My husband took the call from Joey's third-grade teacher when Joey kicked one girl and hollered at another. Kindly, she added that it was not like him and questioned if all was okay at home. *Let the terrible mother self-judgment parade begin.*

After school, I asked Joey what happened before the meeting with his teacher.

"But, Mom, I wasn't trying to kick Breezy."

"Well, what were you trying to do?"

"I was trying to kick Josh."

"Why were you trying to kick Josh?"

"Because he was throwing sand."

"And, Joey, why did you yell at the girl in your classroom?"

"We were in line waiting for the teacher to go over our work, and she got out of line and then tried to get back in."

"Oh, so you're the line monitor?"

"No, there is no line monitor."

"My point exactly."

During our meeting with his teacher, I found out Joey had also been summoned to another class to apologize for saying something unkind to yet another girl. *Does it ever end?*

I asked, "Joey, what did you say?"

"Well, Mom, Lily told me I shouldn't kick girls. So I told her, 'Oh, yeah? Girls are not special! Women ruin men's lives!'" *What kind of mother are you?*

This is where I felt it necessary to inform the teacher that my husband and I were doing fine.

When we got home, Mike and I talked with him, and as usual, Joey was very receptive. He went to school the next day with apology letters. Since he had written "I'll respect you for the rest of my life" to his teacher, we were certain we had taken care of things. That is until the principal called. "Mrs. Williams, I have Joey here. . ." *I wanted to die.*

Joey had gotten sassy with his teacher after being addressed for doing a back flip in the hallway and was sent to the principal's office. *You can forget about that mother-of-the-year award; however, doing a back flip was quite impressive.*

I hadn't had these types of calls with Monica or Tim. Joey was the easy one, the compliant one, the one who said, "Okay, Mommy." How was this happening? Sometimes our first instinct can be to get mad and come down hard on our child when we hear of their misconduct, but somehow I knew that wasn't the way to go. When I got home that day, I locked myself in my room and dropped to my knees and cried out, "God, please help me. Show me what to do with this child."

"In my distress I called upon the LORD, and cried to my God for help; He heard my voice from His temple, and my cry for help before Him came into His ears" (Psalm 18:6). Sometimes when kids act out, what they need is more love and attention, not discipline. What I heard from God was to give Joey patience, understanding, and time.

Think about how, in the book of Judges, Israel cried out to the Lord because of Midian. And God approached Gideon with affirmation: "And the angel of the LORD appeared to him and said to him, 'The LORD is with you, valiant warrior.' Then Gideon said to him, 'O my lord, if the LORD is with us, why then has all this happened to us? And where are all His miracles which our fathers told us about, saying, 'Did the LORD not bring us up from Egypt?' But now the LORD has abandoned us and handed us over to Midian" (Judges 6:12–13). Gideon accused God of abandoning Israel. God didn't chastise him but instead reassured him: "And the LORD looked at him and said, 'Go in this strength of yours and save Israel from the hand of Midian. Have I not sent you?'" (Judges 6:14). Then, the angel of the Lord was patient as Gideon expressed his apprehension and prepared an offering and even more patient as Gideon asked for not one but two fleeces, even after his offering had been consumed by fire. When Gideon was instructed to tear down the altar of Baal, he did so by night because he was afraid. God responded not with anger but with tenderness and patience. Through Gideon's leadership, Israel defeated their enemies.

When your child is struggling and acting out, this is the time to show extra love and understanding. If Monica threw a fit or yelled at us, we'd stay calm and let her express herself. When your impossible kid becomes loud and expressive, it's important to remain calm and steady.

We all make mistakes, and we need to extend our children the same grace and mercy God extends to us. Oftentimes, misbehavior can be corrected by giving our time. By the time Joey entered middle school, calls from the teachers and principal had stopped with more focused time and attention from us.

FAMILY TIME

Not only did we have nightly family dinners, we also instituted Friday Family Night, which still happens. Mike and I have kept Friday nights clear for family time. Starting this tradition when the kids were young, we fully expected they'd opt out when they were teenagers. There was one Friday night when

Joe was saying goodbye to his high school friends, and I asked him where they were going. He told me they were going to get pizza and hang out. Puzzled, I asked him why he didn't go. "Mom, it's Friday night." He seemed a bit irritated with me. "I want to be with you guys." During Monica's eighteenth birthday party, one of her friends made a joke about how she knew not to ask Monica to do anything on Friday nights.

Our kids knew we enjoyed them and wanted them around, and in turn, when the teen years hit, they still wanted to spend time with us. When you make time for your kids, they make time for you. Sometimes, in order to make this happen, you need to pick stuff you know they like and enjoy and invite them to do it with you. Pursue your child and initiate time together.

I can recall one time taking Tim to a coffee shop when he was fifteen, and he had earbuds in his ears and was listening to music. I remember him saying, "It's okay, Mom, I can hear you." Our time together was not about me; it was about the two of us being together. I was entering his world, and at the time, his world was about his music. I accepted him where he was. Tim has continued to make time and space for me throughout his life—without earbuds in his ears.

And I feel like we've circled back to the "Cat's in the Cradle" song—kids need time and to feel like they belong somewhere. Give your impossible kid a place to belong and be heard.

Does this work? Here's an unedited eighth-grade essay Monica wrote titled "Smell the Roses." Please know that during this time, she was driving us crazy and seemed to be fighting with us continually.

Can many people say that talking to their mom is much more fun and easy to talk to than their friends? The relationship between my mother and I is filled with much love. I have lots of respect for her and the way she lives her life. She is an example of how a mother should be. My mother has taught me many lessons about life. She is loving, caring, and understanding.

Although my mother may seem like the most wonderful woman to ever walk the earth, she is not! Like most mothers and daughters, there is confrontation. Fortunately, arguments do not last long with us. One of us will always apologize. Admitting I was wrong, sometimes, is important in our relationship.

We all have hard times in life, and those hard times seem to happen to me all the time. One time, my mom and I started arguing over something. Afterward it got me really upset. I started bawling like a baby. Mom comes in my room and gives me a hug. She just let me cry in her arms. Then my Mom asked me why I was crying. I told her I was really stressed out lately and felt like crying to get it all out, and because I was extremely hungry. My brothers were in bed and Dad was out for the night. So, she told me to get some food and then go into her room. We sat together talking, watching TV, and eating until my dad got home. The relationship I have with my mother plays a very significant role in my life.

Mom has taught me to stop and smell the roses,

literally. I go on walks with her and when we come to a bush of roses, she stops. My mom looks at all of them and smells each one. Then she determines which one smells the best. Mom shows me to notice the little things in life, and to not take little things in life for granted. As a person can see my mom is very energetic.

As a person can tell, I love my mother very much. We have a very special relationship. She has taught me to not be snub. Mom has taught me how to succeed. There is always compassion, when either of us are upset. My mom is a person who has inspired me to become wise with what I do with my life. My mom is a very knowledgeable person. Now, whenever I stop by a rose bush I smell the roses.

I know you may feel like you're losing the parenting battle at times when you have a strong-willed kid. Just today, Monica was over with her little toddler, who earned a time-out and yelled at her and called her names as he sat on his time-out chair. In between my laughs, I told her, "It's okay. You're doing great." I'm saying the same to you. If you've been insulted by your impossible kid today, you're doing great. Carry on, sister.

Therefore, my beloved brothers and sisters, be firm, immovable, always excelling in the work of the Lord, knowing that your labor is not in vain in the Lord.
1 CORINTHIANS 15:58

Again, it's okay to be human. Having to pick ourselves up from time to time reminds us we are human, and humans are messy. And now, my friend, it's time for the sex talk. Feel free to laugh at me.

THE SEX TALK

Thinking about someday having to explain sex to my daughter gave me a significant level of anxiety. To alleviate some of my discomfort, I had the scene all planned out in my head. At the scheduled time for the big talk, calm and peacefulness would fill the room as we sipped hot beverages at the kitchen table adorned with beautiful flowers. I'd be wearing a pretty dress as the sun streamed in through the windows.

It all looked so good and doable in my mind. But this was the reality: Mike was in the garage. Tim was six, running back and forth from the garage, backyard, and into the house. I was in the living room nursing my youngest, wearing a shabby nursing gown. That's when Monica sat next to me with an intensity that showed she had something on her mind.

"Is there something you want to ask me?" I asked.

"Yes," she declared with the confidence of a teenager, even though she was only seven, "I want to know where babies come from."

I gave her my standard answer: "Mommies and daddies get together, and God gives them a baby."

"No, Mom, I want to *know*. I want to know about sex."

Oh no, this can't be happening. I'm in my nightgown!

"Sex is something for married people," I said.

"*Mom*, I want to *know*. Tell me, Mom. I want to know what sex is."

Tim ran in, and when he heard the word *sex*, he ran back

out. Then he went to the garage and told his father he had to get out of the house because "They are talking about sex in there!"

I was still feeding the baby, "Okay, honey. One day next week after school, we can sit down and talk about it."

"No, Mom, I want to know *now*."

"Can't we talk about this next week sometime?"

"*You* don't want to tell me. Mom, tell me! I want to know!"

"Okay, honey, let me finish nursing the baby."

"You don't want to tell me! Mom, I want to know. Tell me."

"Honey, I'll tell you, just let me finish with the baby."

"Mom, tell me. I want to know. You don't want to tell me, do you?"

"Monica, I'll tell you. Just let me finish with the baby and put him down so we can talk."

There was no getting out of it, and if I didn't tell her, she would have probably asked Grandma, and we know how that might go.

After putting the baby down for his nap, I took a deep breath, sat on the couch, and bravely dove in.

"Okay, now before I tell you anything, I want you to know that God says sex is only for marriage, and if you have sex outside of marriage, then you could die." There's my famous line, and I'm not proud of it today, but once again my fears about "what could happen" took over. When she got older, I did explain STDs and clarified my "you could die" statement, but for the moment, dying seemed to suffice.

Then I explained sex to her as simply as I could—and there were hand motions involved. Too much? Maybe.

Then she asked me, "Is it good?"

"Yes, honey, it's great. Sex is a gift from God; He created it, and it's great but only in marriage."

And that was that. She found out what she wanted to know, and she went on her way. And I felt like I had just slid down a long, steep hill, took a few rolls, and landed on my feet completely dazed. *Okay, that's it, I did it.* My other two were boys, and my husband would be handling them, so I was done. Whew! But as you already know, I did throw in my two cents later about dying and penises falling off.

It's important to talk with your kids about this stuff even if you fumble a bit—like me. Ask questions and gently take the initiative. Your child may very well be ready for this talk way before you want to have it. My kids still talk to me about sex so much so that I'll sometimes put my fingers in my ears. I'm not kidding. I even chant la la la la la.

Intentional parenting takes time. They don't want *things*, they want *you*. Time—once it is gone, you can never get it back.

— — — — — — — — — — — — — — —

THOUGHTS FROM MONICA:

My mother's sex education talk is one of the most vivid memories I have from my childhood. Imagine being seven, and your mom is using hand gestures to explain this whole process. I was thoroughly grossed out by the entire conversation. It was odd and awkward, but even then, I was glad to be told the truth. That was something I learned early on with Mom—you could ask her anything, and she would always respond and respond with honesty. But before I tread further: *No*, I will not be telling my children if they have sex before they are married, they will die. *Who tells their kids that?!* My mother, apparently. Every time I hear that story, my eyes roll so hard to the back of my head. That's my mom. She's a little crazy, but at least she's the fun kind of crazy.

Especially as a parent, I can now appreciate the nuance of her parenting. Half of being a mom is staying engaged, leaning in, picking up on cues from your child to help discern what they are going through. But above all, the quality that made a difference for me as a child was that Mom listened.

I absolutely loved, *loved*, our noontime chats. I got to talk, and Mom listened to what *I* had to say. She was engaged and focused on me. Discussions were candid, even with both of my parents. But it wasn't just about the listening. The second aspect to my parents was that I could talk without that often inevitable wave of parental judgment: *"Do this. Do that. Say this. I can't believe you did that! You shouldn't have said that. Here's what you should have done."* Especially during my teenage years, I didn't live with the fear of my parents finding out what was really going on in my life. And that was in stark contrast to many of my friends. I cannot tell you the number of times I would be around one of my friend's parents and hear them say, "She would tell me if she was having sex with him. Oh, they don't lie to me. I know what's going on because we talk." Newsflash: They were having sex; yes, they lied to you; and no, you have no idea what is going on.

I wasn't afraid of my parents. And I would wonder what made my relationship with Mom so different. And here was one huge point I came to realize: Mom was always on your side. I always knew that no matter what trouble I would find myself in, Mom was going to show up and go to bat for me.

My parents didn't make up their minds about a situation before speaking with me. I knew I would be heard, and doubly so, I knew they weren't going to lose it. When I found out that I could make mistakes, go to them with it, *and* they weren't going to "freak out" at me, that changed the whole child-parent relationship right there. And I know the exact situation where I had a mental shift as a child.

When I was in the fifth grade, it was the hardest year I experienced in elementary school. I know how overly burdened that sounds for the life of an eleven-year-old, but it was true. I had poor grades, bad friends, and low self-esteem. And teachers did not make it any easier. After a multiple-class field trip, our three teachers put sixty students into one little bungalow building. They stood at the front of the classroom and proceeded to tell us that we had represented our school poorly on the trip. They were disappointed and disgusted with our behavior, but some of the kids were good while others were bad. Then one-by-one, with each teacher taking turns, they called out and dismissed the "good" kids. I sat there, watching other children leave the room, and I had no doubt in my mind that I would be included with these wonderful kids. I thought through the whole trip, and I honestly couldn't think of what I had done that was wrong. I sat there with my back straight and hands folded in my lap; I just knew I would be called to exit.

The last name was called. It was not mine. My heart sank, and my stomach felt queasy. I wanted to cry. I had never been a "bad" kid, but this situation, the whole school year, I felt like I was bad. The teachers told us we had to write a note to our parents detailing all the things we had done wrong. I didn't know what to write, so I regurgitated what the teachers said. I then folded up my little slip of shame and slid it into my backpack. I was a bad kid, but I didn't want Mom to know that. When I got home, I zipped open my bag, took out my pen, and without that paper ever seeing daylight, I secretly forged my mother's signature inside the backpack and chose to forget about it.

Forget about it, I did. . .that is until the next day, when my teacher pulled me aside to tell me that she noticed it wasn't my mother's writing. I would have to go back home and have Mom sign that scarlet letter of a confession. I hung my head and said I would. I was caught. There was no way around this. But what my teacher didn't know was that I had been forging my mother's signature *all year long.* This was just the first time I got caught.

Later that day, I slunk myself into the kitchen, barely able to bring my head up and look Mom in the face to tell her the horrible truth. "Mom," I said, "I have a note here from school, and I faked your signature on it." A tiny, itsy bitsy moment barely went by, and without missing a beat, Mom replied, "That's fine." *WHAT?! Like seriously! Who are you right now?!* I was flabbergasted. My poor little barely decade-old brain could not comprehend this. I just thought, *To heck with it all, let's tell her the whole truth and see how this goes.* It all came tumbling out how I had been forging her signature all year long and what had happened after the field trip. And at the end of my admission, Mom said, "It's okay. You can sign my signature on anything you need. I trust you." And that was it. I wasn't in trouble. I didn't get yelled at. I wasn't punished. *My mom didn't think I was bad.* And in fact, she was now my accomplice. But more importantly, it was that very day when I discovered I could go to my parents with anything, and they were going to be on my side.

From then on, I wasn't afraid to be honest with them. I didn't have to fear their recourse. All the little chats prior suddenly added up to all the major discussions of what would become a soon-to-be adult life. My life was mine to manage, but Mom and Dad would at least be there to help. Mom was always, and still is, lovingly nosy. Despite all the battles I fought against her, I wanted to matter enough for Mom to wade her way through the cement of my emotional walls and find *me* on the other side.

I learned that Mom and Dad were safe. All that time invested and all those "little chats" from when I was young, they didn't just disappear. They turned into something more. All those times became the loving, trusting, laughing relationship we have today.

— — — — — — — — — — — —

Thoughts to Ponder:

- Have you been allocating your time in the best manner possible?

- Are your children getting the time and attention they need from you?

- Is it time to schedule "dates" with one or all your children?

- Look at your calendar. Does it reflect what is most important to you?

Chapter Five

THE REAL SUPERWOMAN

A superwoman—one who can do it all, have it all, overcome every obstacle. Her kids are always in line, her husband touts her praises, and she has exceptional strength and ability.

We can do it all, and look great, while we deal with poop, snot, and vomit—that's the Superwoman Motto. We think we need to be a stylin' mom through exploding diapers, cuts and scrapes, ABCs, and screaming, "Stop hitting your brother," because we have extraordinary superhuman powers. When our desire meets our reality, we end up crying in the bathtub. We can become out of balance with an endless need to do more and then try to hide any imperfections or feelings, throwing on our superwoman capes, wondering why we don't look better. Well … Superwoman always looked good because she didn't wipe butts or clean vomit off her shoes. What are we striving for anyway—an impossible target to go along with our impossible kid? Take a break already.

In this chapter, you'll hear four of my personal "super-woman" stories, which will clearly indicate how torn and tattered and not sexy my hero cape was as a mom (as if you didn't know that already).

Here's my first "superwoman" story: In the middle of the night, I rushed Mike to the hospital. He had contracted salmonella poisoning from a local chain restaurant. When the health department got involved after he returned home, my life got extra difficult. Before Mike became a pastor, we had owned restaurants, and because of the salmonella diagnosis, he was ordered to stay out of the one restaurant we had at the time. This meant I had to step in and run it until the bacteria was completely out of his system. He was home with the kids, and I was the one heading to work each day, feeling like a little girl in Daddy's shoes, sliding, tripping, and falling. At the end of the workday, he'd have a hot bath waiting for me. I would sit in the tub and cry. He was handling the kids just fine—actually, better than fine. He mastered it and made it look easy. I could give you a list of his faults here, but frankly, running the home in my absence wasn't one of them. I, on the other hand, was melting down regularly. I wanted to rise to the occasion and be superwoman, but I was just barely hanging on, getting through by taking it one step at a time, doing the next thing that had to be done, praying and crying.

While I was at work one day, a call came from my husband, informing me that this arrangement could last a year, maybe two. I told him I had to go, and I rushed to his office (which was a tiny space with a makeshift desk, tall chair, and a cement floor), got on my knees, and sobbed to God, proclaiming, "I can't do this!" I asked if He could please take it away. I had barricaded myself in the office so the employees wouldn't see me falling apart and therefore think I couldn't run the joint. God was merciful, and before the year was up, Mike was cleared and back to work. I don't think I've ever appreciated the job my husband did more. And it was a lesson on trusting God and reconciling doubt and weaknesses.

Throughout my mommy journey, I wanted to portray that I always had it together and could handle whatever life or my impossible kid threw at me. And I wanted to look amazing while doing it. I wanted to believe I had it all together—all the time. I wanted to create a perfect picture for myself and others, and I had a hard time accepting my limitations. My perfect facade would crumble, I'd leak a bit, and then I'd suck it back in because I had to be Mom—I had to be Superwoman.

I liked doing things that looked good on the outside, because it affirmed what I so desperately wanted to believe about myself. But my facade could only last for so long.

Here's my "superwoman" story number two: There was a program at the grammar school my kids attended called "Women in History" for which moms, while in costume, would pretend to be a woman from history and teach the kids. Each year the school handed out the scripts to moms who wanted to participate. My first year, I portrayed Deborah Sampson, who disguised herself as a man to fight in the Continental Army during the American Revolutionary War. I walked in the rooms with a bloody bandage, rifle, and war hat. I made it in the daily paper, thinking my kids must be so proud of me. The next year, I started my research early playing Mary Kingsley, a proper English woman who was a writer and explorer through West Africa during 1893 and 1894. I made it into the paper again that year, as I traveled through the school with my teacup and fancy umbrella. My kids were even prouder of me. The third year, I decided to go all out as I portrayed Queen Elizabeth I and got an authentic costume from the CBS TV station. That year, I made the front page of the paper. *Who's Superwoman now? Huh, kids?*

Most moms read from the paper the school gave them. But oh no, not me, I had to do way more research and memorize my part. I mean, I was the Meryl Streep of Valley View Elementary. An actor must prepare. As soon as the assignments went out, I went to work—reading and studying every piece of literature I could get my hands on, learning my character, and practicing my lines and accents. Dinners were missed; family time was missed—those were luxuries, and I had a job to do.

As my Queen Elizabeth debut wrapped, I was already looking forward to the next year. But there was family mutiny brewing unbeknownst to me. My little darlings went to their father pleading, "Daddy, please help us." A family intervention was soon underway. My husband sat me down with the kids and, as kindly as he could, explained how difficult it was for the whole family when I did my "parts." My Meryl Streep days were over, and I cried. They were right. I knew there was no way I could do the program and have balance too. My three-year-reign was over.

Trying to be Superwoman can look different for all of us. We all have stories.

I must tell you about Paula here. Paula worked hard to be a success in business, and I was visiting her at her beautiful mansion of a home. As I congratulated her for all her accomplishments and admired her gorgeous home, she let me know she spent her Saturdays cleaning it—which included five bathrooms! So, this accomplished businesswoman was scrubbing toilets on Saturdays. I said, "Wait. *You* clean this house?" She nodded. "Have you ever considered hiring a cleaning service?" I asked. The next time I saw Paula, she let me know she had taken my suggestion and hired a service. It was almost as if she needed validation from someone else to enjoy her Saturdays—which she truly earned.

Well, just like Paula, you have earned validation—you're a mom!—and I'd like to stop here and say, "Thank you, thank you, for all you do!" Being a mom can be an endless and thankless job, and sometimes you just need to hear the words *thank you* and *keep up the good work*. You are imprinting generations—keep up the good work!

EMPOWERING OUR KIDS BY BEING REAL

It's okay to get in touch with your human messiness. Have you ever considered that our children need to see normal human emotion? How we deal with "stuff" will teach our kids a great deal. If they do not see us being normal and human, with weaknesses and all, they will not be able to relate to us. When our children see our weaknesses, emotions, and how we work through our struggles and feelings, it shows them they can do the same. Once our impossible kid views us as human and real, we are more approachable.

No matter how hard we try to model trusting God through all life's circumstances, sometimes the pressures of life burst through.

Ready for "superwoman" story number three? The kids and I were on the way to church for a children's event in which my husband would be speaking. Monica was fifteen, Tim was fourteen, and Joey was seven. Before we even left our driveway, I was fighting with Tim over the volume of his Christian rock music.

As we drove, unhappy with the lower volume, Tim turned the music off. Monica and Joey started singing to fill in the silence. Tim yelled at his siblings to stop, and a three-way fight broke out.

I screamed, "Shut up! Everybody just shut up!" It was quiet until Tim turned his music back on. With blasting rock playing, my van suddenly shut down—in the middle of the freeway. I managed to slowly maneuver to a small triangular space between two merging freeways. Panicked, I called Mike. He said, "Honey, just call 911 right now."

Did I listen to him? No. I hung up and just sat there, paralyzed and questioning if my husband's advice was the right thing to do. My phone rang. It was a friend, and I answered with "I have an emergency! The kids and I have broken down on the freeway!"

Elizabeth told me to stay calm and that she would call a tow truck for us. My moment of gratefulness changed to anger toward my husband. I thought to myself, "Why didn't *he* call a tow truck for me?!" Just then, Mike called, and I started in on him, "Why didn't you call a tow truck for us?" He explained the quickest and safest path was calling 911. Which was right.

When we finally arrived at the mechanic's shop, which was down the street from our home, the driver wanted one hundred and fifty bucks in cash. I didn't have a hundred and fifty bucks, and I lost it. . .*again*. Somehow, between me, my children, and my friend, we were able to come up with the money.

After paying the driver, Elizabeth said, "Come on, kids, let's all pray for Mom." In the middle of an empty parking lot, in the dark, holding hands, they prayed for me, yes me, Superwoman.

When he got home, I apologized to Mike and to my children. Modeling trust, kindness, and control for my kids went out the car window at "Shut up! Everybody just shut up!" What a humbling day.

A week later, I had a do-over when our van again shut down on the freeway, and I had a chance to handle things better. With all of life's challenges, we are continually presented with opportunities to be an example to our kids of what trusting God looks like. Don't worry if you blow it; you'll get another chance.

I have so many not-so-proud mommy moments. Perhaps you do too. We can't get caught up in those moments but must instead keep moving and following Jesus one day at a time. In Luke 17:11–19, Jesus was traveling to Jerusalem when ten men diseased with leprosy yelled out for mercy. Jesus instructed these lepers to "go and show yourselves to the priests." To keep everyone at a distance, these men were used to screaming, "Unclean, unclean," when they approached people. And yet, Jesus instructed the lepers to walk to the priests. I'm sure they questioned if going would have any effect, but they moved forward anyway and did what Jesus instructed. The men walked in obedience, one step at a time, and along the way, they were healed. Not one, not two, but all ten were healed, and only one turned back to thank Jesus.

We are all in need of God's mercy. We are all in need of God's healing—physically, emotionally, spiritually. We all desire for God's power to work in our lives. When we run to the feet of Jesus, we tap into God's power. On days where your impossible kid seems to be wearing you down, run to the feet of Jesus with thanksgiving, knowing God will give you the power you need. Keep walking; your victory is coming.

> *Her children rise up and bless her; her husband also,*
> *and he praises her, saying: "Many daughters*
> *have done nobly, but you excel them all."*
> PROVERBS 31:28–29

IDENTITY

As the empty-nest years were approaching, after one of my children had already moved out, I was talking with my daughter and said, "What am I going to do now?"

She quickly replied, "Well, Mom, what do you like to do?"

Not skipping a beat, I said, "I like to spend time with my kids." Then we laughed.

I love spending time with my kids, but as devoted as I was to being a mom, I had multiple activities I did outside of being a mom. In addition to writing, I played league softball with my husband, took piano lessons, went to a gym, went on vacations alone and with my husband, and served in ministry.

Don't lose who you are as a person. As soon as you find your identity as being married to your husband or being a mom to your children, you can lose who you are as an individual. We can't look to our children to get our emotional needs met. God taught me that lesson over and over.

MOTHER'S DAY

And for the grand finale, folks, here's "superwoman" story number four: It was Mother's Day. Joey was six and remembered it was Mother's Day, but my two teens seemed to forget. That stung.

On the way to church, my daughter told us she had a gift for Grandma. What about Mom? Remember me? While at church, I noticed a teenage boy hugging his mom, and I lost it, crying so hard I had to leave. As I sat on the side of the road crying, I had a flashback to 1979, when I was a teenager. It was Mother's Day, and none of us had remembered Mom. She was in bed crying. I recall I couldn't understand why she was so upset. So, Dad and I hit the road to find Mom presents, and when we returned with wrapped gifts, Mom was still in bed. Suddenly, I understood how Mom felt.

After church service, all the younger children were giving their mothers a flower that they had made in class. I started mentally preparing for showing my appreciation to my six-year-old, but my flower never arrived. I asked him, "Joey, where's Mommy's flower?"

Joey said, "Oh, I gave my flower to Nicholas to give to his mother."

What? He gave away MY flower?

"Joey, why did you give Mommy's flower away?"

He said, "Nicholas was under the desk while we were making the flowers, and he didn't have anything to give to his mom."

Oh, so now this kid who made the poor choice to play under a desk gave my flower to his mom.

"But Joey, if you gave away the flower, then you would not have anything to give to your mom."

"Well no, Mom, because I knew we would be here for two services, and I could give you whatever we made in the next service. But Nicholas didn't have anything for his mom."

When we got home after church, I'm embarrassed to say I cried like a baby. My children had no idea what to do. *It had finally happened. Mom went loony tunes!*

One of the kids asked their father why Mom was crying. Mike said, "Mom is hurting. She does a lot for you guys, and she's feeling unappreciated right now."

I continued blubbering, wanting to pull it together but unable to. Then all my children started crying. I felt worse.

My thirteen-year-old son gave me a hug. That would have made my day in itself, but then he told me he was sorry and that he loved me. My other two followed suit. I sobbed. *Guess what, kids? Mom has feelings.* All the while, I kept asking myself if this was somehow an indication of my poor parenting.

After finding out that the child who had been under the table had lost his father the year before, I felt a bit redeemed in knowing Joey had shown love to a hurting boy. Once again, I was shown up by a six-year-old. Thank you, ladies and gentlemen, I'll be here all week. Try the cheeseballs.

*"By this all people will know that you are My disciples:
if you have love for one another."*
JOHN 13:35

As difficult as that particular day was for me, I think in the end we all learned valuable life lessons. I learned that it was healthy to show emotional pain and express feelings, and my kids learned that Mom was not a robot—even though Mom tried to put on the best superwoman show possible. My relationship with my daughter became more tender and warmer after this episode, and I opened up more of my human messiness and was more vulnerable and honest.

RELATIONAL HEALTH

One giant enemy to contentment is comparison. Have you bought into the superwoman myth of an overloaded schedule and an unending to-do list? We can watch others who seem to handle more than we can, and then we wonder what is wrong with us. Instead of comparing and committing emotional terrorism, look for your victories each day. Did you use your "patient mom voice"? On some days, that alone is a huge achievement. Who cares that you didn't shower? Jack ate his broccoli today! You were a hot mess when your husband got home, but you turned into a supermodel when you flashed him your booty when the kids weren't looking. Big win! Count your wins every day.

As you tally your mom wins, consider how you can care for yourself. Sometimes Mom needs a time-out. Take it along with time to reflect and rest. And accept help. Let those kids help with household duties—how can we teach our children to be humble if they have never cleaned a toilet or taken out trash? It's okay to feel tired, and it's okay to accept help.

STEADY WINS THE RACE

There are three life questions that can help you soar through every season:
1. How is your spiritual life?
2. How are you doing emotionally?
3. How are you doing physically?

1. Spiritual Health

How are you and God? If you and God are in a good place, life will seem lighter and brighter. Connect with God each day even if only for two minutes—read a verse, pray, thank Him for your blessings. Even just a little will go a long way with God. Look what He did with five loaves of bread and two fish (Luke 9). Do what you can, and build on the foundation whenever you can.

2. Emotional Health

Are you feeling lonely or overwhelmed? Are you taking time to nurture yourself? If we are on empty, there will not be much, if anything, to spread around. I've heard moms say, "I don't know what's wrong with me." After hearing more about the schedule they're keeping, I'll say, "You're tired. There's nothing *wrong* with you; you're just tired." If this is you, give yourself permission to take a break—somehow.

If you are feeling lonely or overwhelmed, maybe you need

to take time to connect with others. All of us are made for connection. Don't isolate yourself. Satan does his best work when he gets us isolated. We all need trusted people in our lives to say, "Hey, great job," or help reel us in if we have taken a turn down headed-for-disaster lane.

Do you have unresolved conflict in your relationships? Unresolved conflict can give Satan a foothold. It tears you up emotionally and sometimes physically. How are your relationships? Is there a relationship that needs some mending? Maybe you need to resolve something with your husband, a friend, or even one of your children. Our kids need to hear "I love you," but they also need to hear "I'm sorry" and "I was wrong." Those few words are very powerful. Saying "I'm sorry" and "I was wrong" can heal and restore a relationship. It also models humility and humanness.

Above all, accept your feelings. Your feelings are real and valid. And accept and be kind to yourself.

3. Physical Health

Are you taking care of your body? Trust me on this: your future "older" body will either thank you or rebel against you. Fueling your body well and getting out and moving, even if only for thirty minutes a day, will have tremendous benefits. I have found the key with exercise is discovering something you enjoy. If you can't seem to find the time to go for a walk, park your car as far away from the store so you'll have to walk more—every little bit adds up.

Paying attention to your relational health will set you up to be a real superwoman.

WILL THE REAL SUPERWOMAN PLEASE STAND UP?

Can we really be a superwoman? We can if we redefine the term. The real superwoman. . .

- Is human
- Accepts her limitations
- Takes breaks
- Doesn't give up on her impossible kid
- Deals with poop, snot, and vomit and still has a heart filled with love and adoration
- Tucks kids in at the end of a long day
- Falls and gets back up
- Says "I'm sorry"
- Calls out to God for help

Hey there, Superwoman, I love your cape! Now, keep flying, Mom! You're doing splendidly. One day your children will appreciate you and pour back to you all you poured into them. It may not be today, but that's okay. Count all your victories anyway. Keep following Jesus one step at a time.

Therefore be imitators of God, as beloved children;
and walk in love, just as Christ also loved you
and gave Himself up for us, an offering and a
sacrifice to God as a fragrant aroma.
EPHESIANS 5:1-2

THOUGHTS FROM MONICA:

We were really proud of her. Mom was the best mom at Women in History month. But when she tells you that she was obsessed, that is the understatement of the century. Most mothers wore an outfit from a Halloween costume shop and read from a piece of paper. But not our mom. She was committed. As Queen Elizabeth I, she turned every little kid's head. The outfit that she wore was royally orange, embroidered and beaded, and her hair was all done up. Kids were craning their necks out their classroom windows to get a look at my mother. Prior to this, I had watched with Mom a BBC, seven-episode series about King Henry VIII, Elizabeth's father, on VHS from the library, learning how he basically murdered all his wives. Her self-education was well-researched. When she played Deborah Sampson, the part she didn't tell you was that she had teachers play along. She quietly slipped into the back of classrooms, acted as if she were sleeping, and then waited for the teachers to call her "Deborah" before she woke up surprised and startled, and *then* she jumped into her monologue.

You can only admire this type of dedication. She could answer every single question a child asked. She knew it all. And after the third year, yes, we were all done. As great as she was, her mania had made the rest of the family insane. Looking back as an adult, I totally understand her obsession.

Here you are as a mom, specifically a stay-at-home mom, and along comes something that you are not only good at but also trained in. Acting was her passion. Of course, she dove on in. As a mom, you have to have things you enjoy, things that don't always involve your children. I get the obsession. I discovered I loved baking when I became a stay-at-home mom. And as a Type A personality, I have a very specific way in which I like to bake. There has been more than one time when my husband has walked in on me trying to explain to my three-year-old son why he shouldn't have just *mixed* the batter, but rather, he should have *folded in* the chocolate chips. I get it now. I can't do everything or get it all right, but at least I can do the hobbies I like, because this mom thing is exhausting.

You've got to have outlets, but that's easier said than done. Even just trying to find some time with God, what a challenge. At least for me. As I write this, I have a one-year-old and a three-year-old, and half of my prayer life is "Dear God, please help me keep them alive today." While the other half is me sobbing over the mini-devotion I just read on my phone about being stressed by your "little blessings." Heck yeah, I'm stressed! I'm dealing with a three-year-old who just climbed up to the medicine cabinet to try to eat the antacids because he thinks the strawberries on the front indicate it's candy. Then the other one won't stop reaching into the seat of her pants to grab globs of diaper rash cream so she can stick her fingers in her mouth and eat it. Yes, I believe there is a God because my children are still alive. And then in walks hubby from work, who for some strange reason still finds me attractive in my gym clothes and unbathed, looking for a passionate kiss. Truthfully, I'm not always into it. And my point? Superwomen don't exist. I can't do it all, so it's okay for me to be human. It's okay to cry a little in front of my kids and to tell my husband I'm really tired today and to just order pizza.

I learned all this because I learned it from Mom on that fateful Mother's Day oh so long ago, when we all woefully undervalued her. I still remember her completely sobbing at the kitchen table. She could barely utter words. All that came out were rolling tears. And I felt awful. Really awful. She was right; I hadn't thought about her for Mother's Day. But what made this day so significant was that I only recall my mother crying twice before this. To see her weeping, to see her reveal herself as human, was actually quite jarring. Mom had been a superwoman to me. I viewed her as having iron skin. I didn't see her as someone who was emotional. I didn't think I could hurt her feelings, which is why I often tried to hurt her feelings. In my eyes, I didn't think I was getting to her. But as I grew into my teen years, Mom started to show more of herself (or maybe I just started to notice a little more). Finding out she was a real person outside of being a parent was an actual revelation—it was something I needed to learn. Discovering on that day I had hurt her, it taught me Mom wasn't Superwoman. She wasn't the woman of steel. She was a human being deserving of my compassion and thoughtfulness—especially on Mother's Day.

From a once impossible child, it's okay to show your kids you are not perfect—that you cry, that you hurt, that you have feelings. . .that you may have to say sorry for being a little too obsessed about how to mix the cookie batter. It's all part of being a mom. You're doing great. We're doing great. So, let's stand in solidarity and proudly say, "I am a superwoman, and it's okay that I'm not okay."

Thoughts to Ponder:

- Are you trying to live up to the title of Superwoman? Are you ready to give that title a healthier perspective?

- Are you trying to do it all? Is it time to say no to things to make room for the most important things?

- Do you have spiritual, emotional, and physical balance? Is there an area that needs some attention?

- How are your relationships? Do you owe someone an apology? Do you need to seek forgiveness from one of your children?

Chapter Six

BECAUSE I SAID SO

Monica was twelve when she asked, "Mom, is God real?" adding, "I'm not sure if I really believe in Him." My heart dropped to my stomach. In a flash, I began thinking about my shortfalls and mistakes. *Have I not modeled a life that points her to God? Did I mess her up? Where did I go wrong? Why isn't my faith her faith? She has been in church practically every week since she was an infant. How could she even question God's existence?*

I became painfully aware of the many times modeling faith eluded me. Given her persistent and headstrong personality, this was no time for a fake-it-till-you-make-it approach. I knew my words had to line up with my life and what she had seen. Like being faced with a giant bear, I was afraid to move. But I was supposed to know what to say.

I said a quick prayer and took a deep breath. Suddenly, I felt calm, and the words flowed. "I believe He is real; in fact, I am sure of it. But, honey, it doesn't matter what *I* think; what matters is what *you* think. You have to decide for yourself."

Oh, I wanted to say, *God is real because I said so, and that's it. I'm the mom and I know better. Believe it, kid. Period. Now, go play and don't question it.*

Somewhere along the way, I learned demanding and barking orders didn't foster anything good in my kids. How does God parent us? He's loving, guiding us with gentleness and affirmation. Walking with the Lord, I've felt like He's cheering for me. I wanted to parent my kids like this.

My husband and I had an overarching theme to our approach to child-rearing. It's found in Psalm 23:1–4: "The LORD is my shepherd, I will not be in need. He lets me lie down in green pastures; He leads me beside quiet waters. He restores my soul; He guides me in the paths of righteousness for the sake of His name. Even though I walk through the valley of the shadow of death, I fear no evil, for You are with me; Your rod and Your staff, they comfort me."

The rod and the staff brought *comfort*. The Shepherd used the staff to *comfort* the sheep *not* beat the sheep. Nowhere in scripture did the Shepherd beat down or tear down the sheep. His rod and His staff were used to guide, direct, protect, and love. As we parented our children, we focused on doing so with respect and love. At times, our own dysfunction got in the way and we would apologize, but our approach was centered on guiding, directing, protecting, and loving. Offer your child the same respect you want from her. Regardless of age, respect your child's personhood. Ask for hugs, but don't demand. Allow him to say no. Do your best to understand her feelings and preferences. Respect goes a long way—when a child feels mutual respect, he will be more responsive to you.

Upon getting in my car during grammar school pick-up, Monica began to cry as she told me she had been given a take-home slip for bad behavior on the playground. A playground monitor thought she kicked a boy. When she told me which boy, I began to laugh because this kid was almost double her size. I told her right away she wasn't in trouble with me and that I'd head to the school in the morning to find out what happened. After poking around a bit, I found out that she hadn't kicked this boy. It only looked like it from a distance, and the reprimand was erased.

When our son confessed to stealing money from Dad's coin bucket, we listened to *why* he did it. We did not get mad but instead tried to understand his reasoning. He was in elementary school, and Tim became "the hero," buying all his friends goodies from the snack cart. He helped us calculate how much money he had stolen over the course of two weeks. We then made a chart with jobs he could do to earn back the money he had stolen. As he did the jobs, we paid him. Tim put the money in a jar, and when he reached the amount he'd taken, he gave the money back to his dad. Moving forward, understanding how important sharing was for him, I would buy treats he could take to school to share with his friends. Also, I gave him money for the snack cart from time to time. It was important to him to be like the other kids and purchase these items, so I made it important to me, which showed him I valued what was important to him. He never stole money from the coin bucket again.

Instead of blowing up at him, we looked at it from his perspective and tried to understand what was happening in his young life. Then we created a consequence—paying back the money—and we loved him through it.

With permission, I'd like to share a story from my friend, Chris:

"Dad, what do you think was the most important thing we ever did together?" his son asked as they were driving home after his first year of college. Chris reflected on the many memories he had worked to create with his son.

"Was it your coming-of-age celebration at your thirteenth birthday?"

"Nope" was the reply.

"Was it your eighteenth birthday celebration?"

"Strike two."

"Was it the surf trip we had with your buddies and their dads?"

"Dad, I'll give you a clue. It was nothing you planned."

Feeling like he had failed at building a strong foundation for his son, Chris said, "I give up. Tell me."

"Dad, it was the time I got caught stealing Steve's pocketknife, and you had to come pick me up from his house. You didn't judge me. You showed me grace even though I was guilty. And you were the pastor of the church we all attended."

When you discover an infraction or your child tells you about one, remember how God loves you at all times no matter what you do. Most kids don't want to go to their parents when they mess up, because they fear their parents' anger, punishment, judgment, and interference. If your child knows you will come alongside and help—not try to control—they will be more prone to go to you.

Anytime our children came to us confessing something they did, we listened and did our best to understand how they were feeling and what caused the "unwise" choice. We affirmed, expressed our love, and communicated that we were still proud. We would ask what *they* wanted to do about it and how they wanted us to help. We conveyed it was going to be okay, that we would all get through it together. Most of the time, we could tell they had already punished themselves enough with remorse. When someone admits they're wrong, the last thing they need is for another person, let alone their parent, saying it as well. It's like dousing vinegar on an open wound.

If you want her to come to you when she's made poor choices or with questions, you need to establish you are safe and will not overreact. Lavish him with assurance, forgiveness, support, and understanding. Doing this fosters trust. She learns she can trust you. He learns you are safe.

When we accept and love through difficult times, we strengthen our relationship with our children and point them to the Savior. Unconditional love and acceptance are what we always get from God, and when we extend that to our children, we point them to Him.

LIVING THE GOLDEN RULE

Think back to when you were a kid. Now consider Luke 6:31: "Treat people the same way you want them to treat you." What did you want from your parents? Most of us wanted honesty, transparency, kindness, consideration, safety, and to be known and loved. As you parent your impossible kid, remember Luke 6:31. The golden rule applies to parenting if we allow it to, and it can be our gentle guide.

Think about the last time you had to correct one of your children or they came to you with remorse. How did you react? Look at John 18 and how Peter denied Jesus three times. Yet, when Jesus spoke to Peter in John 21 on the Sea of Tiberias, Jesus asked about fish, entreated the disciples to "cast the net," invited, "Come *and* have breakfast," and asked Peter, "Do you love me?" Not once, considering Peter had *denied* Jesus, did Jesus say, "Peter, how could you?"

I know it can be very painful when a child makes poor choices, and we might be tempted to say, "How could you do this to *me*?" If we make it about us, we are in the problem and will have a more difficult time helping our child. There have been times where I have walked through struggles with my kids and waited until I was behind a closed door to let out a deep breath, drop to my knees, and cry out to the Lord. In front of them, I kept a "poker face" because I wanted to preserve their heart and my relationship with them. My grief was my own, not something for my children to bear. Be mindful of the golden rule and what your child is seeing.

LITTLE EYES

*So, as those who have been chosen of God, holy
and beloved, put on a heart of compassion,
kindness, humility, gentleness, and patience.*
COLOSSIANS 3:12

Kids watch everything we do, and it can be a challenge to model kindness and integrity. How do we respond to challenging people? How do we answer tough questions when a little fib seems the easier route? What do we do when we are given credit for something we didn't do? Do we apologize when we hurt or offend others? Do we apologize to our children when we know we were wrong? Modeling grace, honesty, and mercy teaches grace, honesty, and mercy.

One morning while dropping Joey off at his elementary school, in an attempt to save time while fearing that Tim would be late, I drove through the bus loop. I can hear your gasp. I knew it was wrong but did it anyway. There were no buses around. *Whatever.* Joey got out of my car, and an angry school monitor tried to yell something through my car window. I kept driving.

"That was rude!" Tim admonished. "What if everyone drove through the loop?"

He was right. I couldn't *whatever* my way out of this one.

My response: "It was better than saying what was on my mind."

This confession incriminated me more.

Poor Joey got the brunt of it, though, because the lady yelled at him when I drove off. *Great job, Mom.* Tim was right to call me out, and I told him so later. I let my kids know I wouldn't do it again. If we don't acknowledge our slip and own it, we'll be seen as a hypocrite and a phony. This was another story my kids told over and over, adding to the Mom's faux pas list. You can't be perfect, but you can be transparent and real.

If your child sees an inconsistency between your actions and your words, own it. They already know and are probably laughing about it with their siblings—better to let them laugh with you instead of behind your back. We can say anything, but what we do screams volumes. How we handle the relationships within our home models God's design for family—be mindful of what your children are witness to. Does our conduct outside of our home mirror the way we act within our home?

One Sunday, while our family was on the way to church, my husband and I were fighting. After parking, we headed to church looking spiffy in our Sunday best. An elder greeted us with "My, what a lovely family." I smiled and politely said, "Looks can be deceiving." He returned my grin. Just to smile and say thank you seemed way too hypocritical. Give your children honesty. Be honest in front of them. Don't be one way in the car and then another way at church or with your friends. Children can sniff out a fake like a hound dog.

Trying to construct an illusion of perfection can weaken your relationship with your children; being real and openly flawed will build a stronger connection. Children are naturally pure, open, and loving, which is why Jesus said in Matthew 18:2–3, "And He called a child to Himself and set him among them, and said, 'Truly I say to you, unless you change and become like children, you will not enter the kingdom of heaven.'"

I regularly checked in with my children to see if I had injured their hearts in any way by asking, "Is there anything I've done to cause you pain or hurt?" This doesn't mean you erase consequences for poor choices, but it does mean she can go to you with an injured heart. You can apologize for hurting him and still set a boundary. Sometimes our kids would talk with us about a consequence we had set, and we'd change it or take it away if we felt they were right. Have you ever heard "Leaders who can't be questioned do questionable things"?

We allowed our children to question us, and we were open to discussion on all matters. Sometimes we were just straight-up wrong and had to own it and make amends. When a child gives and receives forgiveness, it softens their heart toward our Creator, who forgives lavishly and unendingly.

My dear friend told me that when she visited my home during my childrearing years, she would leave thinking to herself, "Wow, she has an alarmingly open relationship with her kids." We never ceased to surprise her with the way we interacted. She said, no matter their age, my kids could ask me anything, and I would give an answer. They were allowed to listen as we talked, not ever being asked to leave the room. She also noticed that what they thought mattered, they mattered, and their questions mattered; but they were not disrespectful nor did they interrupt.

One who walks in integrity walks securely,
but one who perverts his ways will be found out.
PROVERBS 10:9

Our kids learn more by watching us than by listening to us. There's a story about my grandfather that illustrates walking in integrity. While the kids were home from school due to a snow day, my grandfather walked to work, which was a General Motors roller bearing factory. He walked from East Orange to Harrison, New Jersey, roughly eight miles—in a blizzard. With his car buried in snow, no one knew where he was until he returned home at the end of his workday. When he got home, they asked, "Where were you?" His blatant response, "At work of course." Integrity and faithfulness are caught more than taught.

When we *walk in integrity* and keep promises, we point our children to a Father they can trust. It is so easy to say "Yes, okay, yes!" when our child is persistently bugging us or set a consequence out of frustration, but if we don't come through or follow through, our words aren't worth much. I know follow-through can be difficult with an impossible kid whose liveliness keeps you on high alert. Learning to calmly handle your child's strong-willed nature is key.

THE THREE Cs

When Monica was seven years old, she loved wearing her fancy white cowgirl boots with pink sparkles on the sides. One particular day, we were going to the playground, and I told her to put on her tennis shoes. She refused. I explained I didn't feel it was safe and asked would she please change her shoes. She refused. This escalated to her throwing a fit and screaming, "I hate you!" I told her I loved her and gave her a choice: she could either change her shoes and go to the park or stay home and take a nap—her choice. She continued to yell, "I hate you!" Monica "chose" to take a nap while her brother and I played games at home.

I heard the words "I hate you" more than "I love you" while Monica was growing up. When you hear "I hate you" and then the door slams, it's what you do next that matters most. My instinct was to follow her in and yell at her, but my losing control left no room for reason and restitution. *Breathe.*

Your child needs you to be the parent. You set the emotional temperature of your home. Be the calm in the storm. I like to call this the three Cs. Calm. Clear. Control.

1. Calm. Stay calm. It is never a good idea to fight with a three-year-old or a nine-year-old or a seventeen-year-old. You do not need to engage in an argument with your child. Take a deep breath and be the adult, be the parent. Investigate situations before jumping to conclusions. My friend Ashley found her son drinking out of the chocolate syrup carton. As she probed, she found out there was only a little syrup left in the carton, and he had filled it with milk. Before we react, we need to inquire and listen. Ashley praised his innovativeness when another parent may have reprimanded. But which reaction builds our relationship with our child?

2. Clear. Be clear on your directives: "If you do not put on your tennis shoes, we will not go to the park, and *you* will *choose* to take a nap." Be clear and concise, and then follow through. Just because she's throwing a fit doesn't mean you should.

3. Control. You are in control. Be in control of yourself and the situation. Don't lose your cool. No matter how loud he screams or how many times she proclaims her disdain for you, be calm, clear, and in control. *Breathe.*

When things in your home begin to escalate, stop and be the leveler. Do you want to knock your child off-balance during her next rant? Put on some music and start dancing. Sit down and read a book or your Bible. Invite him to bake cookies with you. I recall hearing, "Mom! Don't you care that I am upset?!" Reply, "Of course I care, but I will not engage in this unhealthy form of communication. When you calm down, we can discuss it." Then, I waited. Calmly. This takes time, and you may be late for things here and there, but it's worth it in the long run. Don't get caught up in her drama. If all else fails, anytime you feel you can't practice being calm, clear, and in control, drop and pray.

LIVING FAITH

One of my regular prayers was that God would make me the mom my kids needed. Pray you will be the mom your child needs *today*. When we stay connected to God, our rock, our fortress, and our strength (Psalm 31), His pouring flows to us and overflows to our kids. Like Jesus said in John 15:4, "Remain in Me, and I in you." When we remain in the Lord, He will guide us and lead us.

Going back to the opening question of this chapter, "Mom, is God real?" I'm glad Monica talked with me about her doubts. It's healthy for your children to question what they believe. Be ready to listen and answer questions. Children are born with a yearning and desire to know God. Part of children's belief process includes wrestling to own their own faith. Even so, Monica's wrestling alarmed me. I thought if I taught her about God, she would automatically believe. Bedtime consisted of nightly devotions from the time my kids were so young they called them "oceans," and we made talking about God and faith a common theme in our home.

I ignorantly assumed she would never question if God were real. At the time of her question, oddly enough, I had never shared my coming-to-faith story with my daughter nor had I ever shared it publicly. Modeling faith is not an easy task, but we can talk about our own story with our kids. It is very powerful for your kids to hear how Jesus changed your life. It is powerful for them to hear about what you were like before Jesus came into your life. Obviously, if your life resembles that of Rahab's, you may need to edit yourself to be age appropriate. Sharing your past can be a bonding time, one that bonds you together and one that bonds them to Jesus.

During the time Monica was wrestling with her own beliefs, I started a Bible study for fifth-grade girls in my home. We called it Girls' Club, and we met weekly. I felt led to start this study but had no idea if there would be any interest. I was shocked to have a house full of girls on our first night. My lesson would be my coming-to-faith story, and as I stood in front of the sea of faces, including my daughter's, it felt like my heart was going to pound out of my chest.

Breathe.

And then I shared my story. . .

> When I was your age, I had a giant attitude.
> I was the kind of girl your mother probably
> wouldn't want you to hang around. I was a
> hurting kid, and I felt alone in a big world.
> I didn't believe in God because my father
> didn't believe in God. I had trouble sleeping
> as a kid because I feared dying. My dad was
> an atheist who taught me there was no God
> from the time I was three. He would tell me,
> "When you're dead, you're dead. They put
> you in the ground. You didn't know anything

before you got here, and you're not going to know anything after you leave here." Because I was young and idolized my father, I believed him. Like most little girls, I thought Dad was always right, and he *usually* was.

The problem was I felt this overwhelming emptiness deep in my heart. I figured that when I got married, when I started a family, when I had a successful career, this emptiness would go away. After getting married and still feeling just as empty, I realized there was no worldly thing that could fill this emptiness in my heart. I started pondering the idea of God but quickly dismissed the notion because *Dad said there was no God, and Dad is always right.*

Then one day, while in my early twenties and newly married, out of desperation I sent a prayer off to the "God who didn't exist." *Lord, I don't believe You are there, but if You are, would You please show me?* Then God revealed Himself to me in ways only God can for each person.

A pastor and his young wife moved into our building. We became friends, and I had someone to ask my many questions. I read a book about Jesus, which fascinated me. Dad had never really talked about Jesus.

The book was *More Than a Carpenter* by Josh McDowell, and this book brought me to the conclusion that Jesus was either a liar, a lunatic, or He was Lord. Either Jesus knew He wasn't God and lied about it; Jesus thought He was God but was crazy; or Jesus *was* God and Lord. This made me wonder what my dad believed about Jesus, so I asked him one day, "Dad, I know you don't believe in God, but what do you believe about Jesus?" My dad replied, "Oh, Jesus was here, that's historical fact." This was unbelievable to me—*My dad, the atheist, believes Jesus was here!* This was almost too much for my brain to comprehend. "Okay, so you believe Jesus was here, but what do you *believe* about Jesus?" What he said next is etched in my memory like I heard him say it yesterday: "Jesus got off the cross and went to China."

I was thinking, *What?! Did I really just hear that? Jesus got off the cross and went to China!? Dad's wrong! My dad, who's always right, is wrong this time. He's wrong! I've spent my whole life not believing in God based upon the theory that Jesus got off the cross and went to China?!*

Suddenly God *was* real. I believed in God. I knew what I believed now and realized I needed to do more than just believe. God wanted more from me. He wanted more than just my belief; He wanted my life.

Now girls, I am going to tell you something

I have never told anyone before. I was twenty-three years old. I got down on my knees in my living room and asked Jesus to come into my life and in my heart. I felt a huge burden lifted off my shoulders, and that empty spot I had all my life was gone. God filled that empty spot. I committed to live my life for God from that day forward, and it has never been the same.

The room was silent. As I peered out at the girls, I noticed my daughter crying in the back of the room. As we transitioned to our next activity, Monica walked over to me. She said, "Mom, I know God is real now. I know He is real because you said so, and you wouldn't lie." The way we live our lives reveals to our children what we believe about God.

— — — — — — — — — — — — — —

THOUGHTS FROM MONICA:

I vividly remember my phase of doubt in God's existence. At twelve, I was in the midst of a serious existential crisis. I remember feeling utterly perplexed at the notion of an alpha-omega being; I remember asking loads of questions; and I remember that no one lost their cool about it. And what I was ultimately left with was the concept that it was acceptable to question my faith. I was not met with shock or dismay or even correction. I was free to make up my own mind, and this feeling has remained with me into my adult years.

I've never walked away from my faith, nor do I try to

remain rigid in it. From childhood, I learned I needed to challenge what I believed. I needed to take my faith and press it hard to the fire, because it is with this flame that we can be molded and grow as believers. God cannot make me better if I never open myself up to the possibility that I may be wrong. And I can admit—I'm wrong a lot.

One story that has stuck with me was the whole boots and playground debacle. I was deeply offended when Mom inserted herself into dictating my wardrobe. Truly, I was personally accosted. How dare she order me around! Who did she think she was? My blood boiled. Screaming, arguing, crying, and yelling "I hate you"—yup, I totally remember that story. I also remember the excellent nap that followed. But life is not without irony, because my son has recently moved into calling me a "bad mom" because I told him to brush his teeth. He's even become more proficient and effective with his insults because he now calls me a "baddie" when I do something he doesn't like. Why stick with two words when one will sum it up perfectly? I have to admire his efficiency.

All those years of saying "I hate you" to my parents actually prepared me for a son who would do the same. Does it hurt my feelings? The first time it did, but now I just laugh. I was him. I get it. He is allowed all his feelings, the good and the "baddie."

But when it comes to parenting, this one thing I am proud to have adopted from my parents: the ability to apologize to my children. Receiving a genuine apology from Mom meant that my feelings and how I was treated mattered. My personhood counted. And although I wouldn't have eloquently described it that way as a kid, I can tell you it was an instant sense of relief to hear "I'm sorry." It brought down my defenses and absolved internal anger. It meant Mom wasn't going to pretend she was right all the time. And as a mother now, I see when I apologize to my son, it provides him an opportunity to give grace, to be kind. I know he's learned graciousness when he responds, "It's okay, Mom."

And let me just say, I felt so cool that it was *my* mom who hosted at *my* house an official girls' night. Those weekly nights were so much fun and impactful. That first evening when Mom shared her testimony, it left an impression with me. Her story made an impact then, and it's continued to do so. Knowing her roots as a believer shaped how I viewed God. And what has always continued to strike me was how she made such conscious choices to not repeat the dysfunctional patterns from her childhood. Knowing from a young age what God had done in her life, it made Him more real to me. It showed me that if this supposed eternal, powerful being could take my mother from a hopeless and self-focused life and turn her into the loving, sacrificial person I knew today, then there had to be some type of truth to what she said. Knowing that God could make actual change in someone's life, it was just what I needed to hear at twelve.

Growing up, everyone had the freedom to be who they were—negative parts included. It fostered a sense of openness and mutual respect. It didn't always look perfect, but it was at least real. Because as a kid, you're still learning how to be yourself in the world, and the world isn't always accepting of who you are. But at least home was safe. At least Mom and Dad were safe. And in turn, it meant Jesus was safe. Even now, my two brothers and I range from biblically conservative to biblically liberal. And I love that about us. Everyone has a different faith journey. As an adult, I certainly appreciated the freedom to explore and question and still receive unconditional love; there is no better picture of who Jesus is than that right there.

— — — — — — — — — — — — —

Thoughts to Ponder:

- As you reflect on your own upbringing, are there things you'd like to emulate? Are there things you'd like to avoid?

- Do you feel like your children see your words and your actions lining up?

- Have you shared your coming-to-faith story with your children?

Chapter Seven

JOINING YOUR CHILD'S DANCE

Walking home from kindergarten with my sweet, precious little Joey, I found that this inflexible child would not hold my hand. I had fond Mommy-memories of holding hands with Tim as we walked all the way home. "Joey," I said, deciding that if I confronted this obstinate five-year-old, I could recreate my warm memories, "your brother used to hold my hand all the way home when he was in kindergarten." Joey replied, "Mom, I'm not Tim! I'm a different kid." Touché! And that's a point for the five-year-old, folks.

Each time I thought, "Okay, I think I have this parenting thing down," one or all my kids would do or say something that would show me I was wrong. . .*again*. We need to be willing to change and grow with our kids, keeping in mind each child's unique design. Know your children. Know your family. Pray for them, and ask God to reveal to you how you can embrace the flow of your child—their unique dance.

Have you ever considered that your children study you? They study your habits. They know your weaknesses and what makes you smile. They watch your mistakes. Children are experts at knowing their parents. If we are to understand our children, we need to be expert studiers of them.

My husband once met with a family in which the parents were convinced their young son was possessed. The boy would yell and scream obscenities and say he wanted to stab himself. He displayed this behavior in my husband's office, and the parents became visibly shaken and began to cry. Mike calmly looked at the child and asked, "Noah, do you really want to hurt yourself?"

Suddenly, the ranting stopped. "No," he responded. Then Mike asked this young boy to step out for a moment. "Your son is not possessed," Mike tenderly told these concerned parents. "He is manipulating you." This child was controlling his parents by having these episodes and then getting whatever he wanted.

How about you? Are your children controlling or manipulating you? Impossible kids have a way of "running" us. If you are curtailing your behavior, maybe it's time to set clear limits and consequences. Sometimes children act out because they need more attention. Ask yourself, Is my child acting out to be noticed?

Study your children. Do you know what motivates them? How about what discourages them? What's important to them? What are their natural leanings? Children are expert students of their parents; we need to be even better students of our children. Just for fun, ask your children a series of questions about yourself, such as:

- How can you tell when I'm upset?
- What makes me sad?
- What is most important to me?
- What makes me happy?

My guess is you'll get a very telling earful. Observing your children and getting in the flow of what makes them tick will help guide you in your parenting. Decisions that may have been right for one child may be terrible for another. I learned this the hard way.

Monica had a wonderful experience with her kindergarten teacher, and I requested the same teacher for Tim. In the process of patting myself on the back for being a proactive mom, I soon discovered I failed to consider their differing personalities. As a result, Tim's first year was horrible—and I was the brilliant mom who requested this teacher. Add this to my Mommy *oops* portfolio.

All we can do is learn and grow with our kids, right? When our youngest was five years old, Mike and I thought it would be fun to coach a T-ball team. We asked Joey if he wanted to play on the team, and he said yes. During the games, however, while Mike and I were both on the field "coaching," he would make a big announcement, broadcasting, "I'm tired." Then he would proceed to the dugout, take off his cleats, and lie down on the bench. Here's the instant replay: Mike and I would be on the field coaching the other kids while ours was prostrate in the dugout!

It didn't take us long to figure out that sports were not his thing, and we didn't get mad or irritated with him. The rest of the family played competitive sports, but we did not mock Joseph for not doing the same. We celebrated his being different. . .and smart. Taking off his cleats was a nice little twist to ensure not returning to the field—quite inventive for a five-year-old. Embrace your children for who they are; don't fight it.

GOD'S MASTERPIECE

We are all one of a kind. God has created each of us to be unique. There is no one else like you, and there is no one else like your child. We are "awesomely and wonderfully made" (Psalm 139:14).

In a family, we need to honor and value each other and respect our differences, celebrating the variations God made in each of us. When we are loved and accepted for who we are, we are given the freedom and ability to change and grow into our full potential. Children will flourish in an atmosphere of unconditional acceptance, love, and approval. Let them know you are not going to love them more because of something they do or don't do. Isn't that how God loves us? His love for us is not based on anything we do. Our children are worth more than material possessions, goals, awards, touchdowns, lead roles, or achieving valedictorian. Be intentional about showing love that is not based on performance or accomplishments.

Here are a few examples:

- Correcting him after a game on the way he played. Instead, praise him for his good example and attitude.

- Getting upset when she brings home a B or lower, even though she worked really hard. Your relationship with her and her relationship with God are more important than her grades.

- Sending him to school when he is sick. Health before school.

- Pushing her to excel at a sport. I know of a family where Dad "strongly persuaded" each of his four kids to play the sport *he* liked. His kids resented him for it.

When Monica was eleven, she was playing in a softball championship game where the kids were feeling pressure to win. Before the game, I sat her down and did her hair, which gave me time to talk with her while I curled said hair. I affirmed her for who she was and not because she made the playoff game. "Sweetheart, you look so cute," I said as I finished. "I did your hair today because, whether you win or lose, I want you to remember you are cute, and no one can take that away. So, win or lose, you'll still be cute." I was lightening the pressure. It was my way of letting her know that when the dust settled, she was worth more than any softball game.

Anytime our children played in any sport or competitive game, we always made it clear we were more concerned about their attitude, character, and conduct than we were about their ability. By all means, compliment their abilities, but don't forget to praise their exemplary conduct. Say something like "You played a good game today. I was particularly impressed with your good attitude. You displayed God's love today when you noticed Katie was discouraged and sat next to her. I am so proud of you."

When our children lost a competition or sports game, we'd often go celebrate. We don't need to win to celebrate— celebrate their effort, celebrate their attitude, celebrate them.

Your children will learn more through disappointments than through victories. The ability to lose well is an art you can teach. Most people have more losses in life than wins, more no's than yeses, more letdowns than successes. True success is defined by the capability to pick yourself up, learn, and then move forward. Teach your children how to move onward and upward. A loss can be a great teaching tool and an opportunity to lavish your children with affirmation.

DID YOU KNOW?

Did you know that Bill Gates, founder of Microsoft; Steve Jobs, founder of Apple; Oprah Winfrey, entrepreneurial mogul; and Mark Zuckerberg, founder of Facebook, all dropped out of college? Anna Wintour, editor-in-chief of *Vogue*, and Daymond John, CEO and founder of FUBU from the show *Shark Tank*, never went to college.

It's all a matter of how we look at a situation. Sometimes, all we need to do is reframe the scene. In the heat of dealing with what seems impossible, look at it from a different angle or perspective. What we do when the heat is turned up will either balance the scenario or turn it into an explosion.

For instance, when our toddler hurled meat across our dining table while guests gasped, we laughed—for weeks. It wasn't a regular thing and therefore didn't need to be addressed.

In the heat of things, stop and ask yourself:

- Do I need to tackle this now?

- How important is this?

- Does this situation warrant my getting flustered?

- Is it best to address this later, when we are not on vacation, when we don't have company, or when we are not having a rough day?

- Do I need to pray about this before I react?

- Am I caught in my child's web and therefore can't help him out of it?

- What will this look like in ten or fifteen years?

I can assure you this same meat-throwing child, now an adult, has very good table manners. In the scope of the big picture, it was not a big deal.

ALLOW SCRIPTURE TO GUIDE YOU

Another extremely effective reframing skill is using scripture. Memorize key verses and apply them:

- When you discover your little darling has poured nail polish all over your new carpet and has carved his signature into your coffee table, say, "Set a guard, LORD, over my mouth; keep watch over the door of my lips" (Psalm 141:3).

- When your child throws a fit because the slushy machine was broken, and you must drag him home for three blocks while he continues with his tantrum, say, "He gives strength to the weary, and to the one who lacks might He increases power" (Isaiah 40:29).

- When water-boy toddler puts his head in the toilet for the third time in one day, say, "Trust in the LORD with all your heart and do not lean on your own understanding. In all your ways acknowledge Him, and He will make your paths straight" (Proverbs 3:5–6).

- When you discover your child has covered the dog with cream cheese, say, "Looking only at Jesus, the originator and perfecter of the faith" (Hebrews 12:2).

- When your talented acrobat hangs from the ceiling fan and crashes down, leaving everything in shambles, remember, "You know this, my beloved brothers and sisters. Now everyone must be quick to hear, slow to speak, and slow to anger" (James 1:19).

If you're wondering, I did not make up the above scenarios. My children played out each one of these lovely escapades. Reframing and taking a pause are very effective and can get you through seemingly impossible circumstances.

I remember the day I parked at my children's elementary school to get a glimpse of what they were like on the playground. I witnessed in horror as my ten-year-old son, Tim, played a game in which he was throwing numerous little girls to the ground. He would run, grab a little girl, toss her to the ground, and then run, grab another, and on and on. I felt mortified as I watched girls dropping like flies. As I went home and stewed, my thoughts went from *What a terrible mother!* to *What am I raising?* and *I'm going to let him have it when he gets home!*

But then God whispered. Have you ever noticed when God speaks to us it's often in a tender whisper? Looking at 1 Kings 19, God approached the prophet Elijah softly—God was not in the roaring wind, the earthquake, the fire. He was in the "gentle blowing." God showed up with a whisper.

When we are feeling frantic and life seems crazy and out of control, we need to stop, be quiet, and listen for God. "Stop striving and know that I am God," says Psalm 46:10. Be still. Cease striving. Listen for God.

Suddenly, my demeanor changed. I began to think about Tim's kind and compassionate heart. I witnessed him giving away his things many times to others. Classmates' moms had told me he was kind to their daughters and often gave compliments about their pretty dresses. Teachers often told me he helped the other children with schoolwork.

So, why would he act in such an appalling manner? I decided to talk with Tim after school. Sitting him down, I told him about what I had seen. As we talked, it became clear he didn't realize how bad his behavior was with the girls; to him, it was merely a fun game. He played that way with his older and tougher sister and didn't see the difference. After explaining it to him, he changed the way he played—and I know because I checked. This same child is a pastor today with the same tender heart.

When we seek to understand our child, we are less likely to jump to incorrect conclusions. While leading a small group for teenagers, one of the girls said her mother had frantically accused her of doing drugs one morning because her eyes were red. Melissa exclaimed, "Mom! I am not on drugs! I was up late doing homework. If you don't believe me, I'll pee for you."

If you're tempted to overreact, ask questions and listen. Also in 1 Kings 19, Elijah vocalized his despair and exhaustion to God, and God was understanding and patient. Elijah said, "I have been very zealous for the LORD, the God of armies; for the sons of Israel have abandoned Your covenant, torn down Your altars, and killed Your prophets with the sword. And I alone am left; and they have sought to take my life" (1 Kings 19:14).

Elijah had been running from Jezebel. He was scared, lonely, and weary. He was not being disrespectful to God, nor was he disobeying God. Our compassionate and loving Father gave Elijah instructions regarding which kings to anoint and who to anoint as Elijah's successor. Obeying God once again, Elijah did all God had commanded him. Later, God did one of the most amazing things in the Bible: "Then Elijah went up by a whirlwind to heaven" (2 Kings 2:11). And let's not forget about the chariot of fire!

Looking at God as the perfect parent, there is much we can learn. We need to listen and understand what is going on with our kids and not jump to conclusions. Seek to comprehend what is happening in their world and look at their heart. Oftentimes, we are ready to take on a battle when really they are just tired or need a little compassion.

And when you have an impossible kid, you have enough battles. Being understanding and providing choices helps him feel responsible, creating a receptive nature. So many things about a young person's life are dictated by others, so when choices are given, it softens an impossible kid.

CHOICES

We would not give Monica advice but would encourage her to make her own decision. "What do *you* think?" and "What do *you* want to do?" are questions we asked. When we force our own agendas, we hinder our children's growth and development. When we guide them to make their own decisions, good or bad, they will learn. In that process they develop character.

Choices communicate trust and affirmation. Mistakes are opportunities to love your children through it, which in turn builds trust. The balance between rules, boundaries, and freedom is a delicate one. We want to give fair and reasonable limits; however, we do not want to restrain them from becoming all God designed them to be. Making decisions, failing, making mistakes enable them to grow and learn. Don't be afraid to let them fail. Just make sure you are there to help pick them up.

Being open to their ideas, thoughts, and opinions, even when different from yours, builds the relationship. My children have taught me quite a bit over the years. Our world changes fast, and at times our children understand our culture in a more relevant way. Let them keep you up to date on what is happening in their world and how they see themselves fitting into that world. This does not diminish the wisdom we possess or our parenting authority. When we let our children teach us a few things, it bridges the gap between us and the culture in which they are growing up.

Keep in mind that some days require more grace than others. Be more graceful on days where there has been more conflict in the home. Give an extra dose of compassion and sensitivity. Keep demands to a minimum. Permit more play or enjoyable activities. Don't make a fuss about uneaten vegetables, grumpy words, or messy rooms. "I know things have been kind of crazy today, and I'm sorry about that. How about we clean up our rooms tomorrow?" Acknowledge their feelings as well as your own.

PRACTICAL STEPS AND KEEPING AN OPEN MIND

Your children may come home from school with an attitude. Instead of getting mad, ask them what happened at school. If they don't respond, say something like "I sense some sadness from you; can we talk about it?" Perhaps they experienced a big disappointment or got teased. If you observe one of them dawdling after you've given a command, ask, "What are you supposed to be doing right now?" Give them a chance to go in the right direction. Create an atmosphere where children can share their feelings. Ask:

- How can I help you?
- How are you feeling?
- What do you need from me?
- Are you unhappy?
- Is there something you need to tell me?

Often, when I'd inquire how Monica was doing and ask questions, she'd become aggressive and belligerent, protesting and carrying on. "Why do you always think I am doing something wrong?" she would holler. "You think I'm stupid!" Later, I'd inquire, "Honey, what is going on? Why did you get so upset?" As we talked, it usually boiled down to her feeling like she had disappointed me in some way or had somehow failed. I would assure her I was very proud of her and that I was her biggest fan.

If you strive to understand your children's world, even arguments and disagreements can enrich your relationship. Help settle conflicts by sharing your heart and your love. When you connect with your children through being vulnerable and real, it gives them a chance to see your heart and your motives. The greater the relationship, the less likely they'll be to rebel.

If your children are acting up, show up. When you need to enforce a rule or give consequences for violating one, show the same amount of love and attention or more attention. When children are struggling, that's when they need extra compassion and support. It's a natural tendency to pull away from your children when they are being unruly or breaking set boundaries, but that's when staying close is most necessary and when they need you most.

It is very difficult for children to continue being rebellious and defiant when you are consistently giving them kindness and tenderness. You may not see results immediately, but over the long haul, you will see the benefits of your choice to parent with intentionality and persistence.

Here are some scenarios of how this can play out:

Scene I: Let's say your six-year-old is more unruly and wild on a certain day. Breaking a clear family rule, he intentionally lets your dog out of the backyard. Hours later, you retrieve Bowzer from doggie prison. What you'd really like to do is put your little tyrant child in doggie prison, but instead you sentence him to a ten-minute time-out. Enforce the limit and the consequence for violating that limit, but when time is up, extend grace by taking Bowzer and your mischief-causer on a walk. Stop for ice cream on the way home. Spend some time talking about what happened, how it affected you, and how you trust he will not do it again. Children will rise to the level of our expectations and belief in them.

Scene II: Your twelve-year-old son gets sent home early from school for making fun of another student. You get a call from the principal, and you cancel your lunch plans to pick up your little darling. When you arrive at the school, you would really love to express your disapproval loudly, but instead you smile, thank the school staff, and give your son a hug. The hug communicates your support and love. It also says you are not ashamed of him.

Then invite your child to lunch. Take him to his favorite restaurant. When you sit down, look in his eyes and say, "Okay, tell me what happened." Allow him to talk. You listen with no judgment, condemnation, or anger. Ask what he could have done differently. Ask him to imagine what the child who was teased must have felt like. After lunch, maybe on the way home, let him know the consequences for his unwise actions.

It may go like this: "I love you, and I am a bit surprised by your actions today. I know you're a great kid and normally would make better choices. This is how it is going to go down. You will write letters of apology to your teacher, the principal, and the student you made fun of. In addition, you will write me a two-page essay on respecting and loving others. And by the way, until it is done, you will not be allowed to play video games or watch TV. This will give you time to get those assignments done."

Scene III: You arrive home early to find that your sixteen-year-old daughter, who has her driver's permit—not a driver's license—took your car without permission to see her boyfriend. As she pulls in the driveway, you are torn between screams of joy, moans of relief, or rants of fury.

Stay calm and express your concern for her safety. Let her see whatever sadness this situation causes you to feel. Refrain from anger; it will only escalate things. When all the engines have cooled down, sit with your daughter and lay out the consequences. Whatever the projected date was for her to receive her license, extend it by a few months. Sign her up for traffic school and attend the class *with* her. Going along shows support and love. It will give you time to talk with your daughter. Also, take her to an auto salvage yard, and talk to her about the lives that were lost or changed. Make sure to talk about the family members who mourned their loved ones. Again, this gives you time together. In all of this, add lunches and dinners to your "road trips." Lastly, invite her boyfriend over to your house more so you can keep an eye on the relationship.

HITTING HOME

At the close of Joseph's first year in high school, he was at the top of his class and then brought home the first fail on a report card our family had ever seen. We had been accustomed to straight As from him. We didn't get angry; we simply asked, "Okay, now what?" After we talked, Mike and I went to the school with him and sat down with his teacher and the principal to help him decide his next course of action. Together with his agreement, he was placed in a make-up advanced placement English class to replace the F. Not only did he end the semester with an A, but he also received affirmation from his teacher regarding his superb writing and received affirmation from us as he overcame this obstacle. This ordeal developed and built his character *and* improved my prayer life. It was not an easy time, but we weathered it together.

In elementary school, Tim was a victim of bullying. I took him to the community boxing center and let him watch as they trained. Then I asked him if he wanted to learn to box. He made the choice to join the boxing program. The best part of this decision was he never was picked on again, and instead he would stick up for others who were bullied. He was in the local paper for winning matches, and no one wanted to mess with him. He could have pursued the Olympics or professional boxing, but he chose to go into ministry. This process of allowing him to be part of the solution developed stamina and character, qualities one definitely needs in ministry.

Monica was really hard on herself when it came to school and grades. She announced one day while doing her homework, "School is not my best subject." One time she called me crying in the middle of the day because of a bad grade on a test. Mike and I broke into the chorus of "Tomorrow" from the movie *Annie*. It was quite bad—neither of us can sing very well. I can't remember if she was laughing, but Mike and I were. This was our way of helping her to lighten up and not be too hard on herself. This may sound a bit insensitive on our part, but we knew she needed more lightheartedness at the moment. When she got home that day, we supported her in mapping out a plan for success in that class.

When Monica was fourteen, she went through a particularly rough patch, being overly obstinate and aggressively argumentative. Each day felt like its own roller-coaster ride. Mike and I bought her a lavish bath set and left it on her bed with a heartfelt note from her dad. What we never told her was this was planned, and we talked about what would make the most impact to express our love. We decided hearing from Dad would be the best course of action for our teenage girl. She cried when she found the gift and read the note. Then she asked, "Why are you guys being so nice to me?" She was being difficult, and she needed us to lean in not lean out, and even though she was pushing us away, we stayed on the roller coaster and were as loving as possible.

God has commissioned you to raise His child. No matter how inadequate you feel, God asked you to do the job. Be faithful, ride the roller coaster, join the dance.

— — — — — — — — — — — — —

THOUGHTS FROM MONICA:

Five-year-old Joe lying face down on the dugout bench lacking any footwear is, hands down, in my top five favorite family stories. I remember I would be in the dugout trying to get him to go back, while looking for my parents, who were out in the field corralling nineteen other tiny human beings—it doesn't get much funnier than that. But that was Joe. He marched to the beat of his own drum.

All three of us were starkly different from each other, and that was embraced in our home. We each had our own likes, interests, and sense of individuality. My uniqueness was fostered. I know that to be true because I was this odd little tomboy growing up. And I'm not putting myself down here. I was a peculiar bundle. For example, I loved sports. I played softball from childhood all through high school; while in middle school, I was in the "Turkey Bowl" football game with the boys; and also, I happened to win the arm-wrestling championship. You would be guessing correctly that I didn't date much in my teens.

I never felt pushed or prodded into things or felt as if I had to be the best. It was always emphasized that character had far more value than winning. And that was the ultimate point I gleaned from my mother curling my hair before the championship games. It wasn't about my looks. Her point was that I was in control of me. A championship softball game was not going to define me. I defined who I was, how I responded to situations, how I treated others. She didn't care if I won or lost, and in classic Mom spirit, she also made the point that you need to have a little fun in stressful situations.

Once I hit middle school, I was making my own choices about my life. Sure, Mom and Dad were always there and available, but the classes I took, the extracurriculars I chose, the friends I made, they were my decisions. Truly, had they stepped in more and chose things for me, I would have completely rebelled. And that is not an exaggeration. If I felt as if they were controlling me, I would have balked and then just gone and done my own thing. The ability to have ownership of my life provided me the margin to actually care about my life.

I distinctly remember in high school, lying in the middle of the living room floor, crying my eyes out that I could not pass geometry class despite studying for hours and also getting help from the teacher. After Mom and Dad comforted me, they laughed, sang songs (not a joke), and told me they knew

I would figure it out. And yes, I did pass Geometry but only by an act of God. I was in the F range when the teacher's computer entirely crashed, clearing out all the students' grades. The teacher had to make up from memory what our grades were. I passed the class with a C.

Growing up, grace was a far bigger deal than achievement. One of my dad's cliché parenting lines was "God gave me grace, so I'm going to give you grace." Which basically meant either he waived any consequences, or I got out of grounding sooner than promised. This statement still makes me laugh, and its impact remains.

During a difficult teen season when my parents "were my enemy," I went walking into my room to find a present resting in the threshold with a letter on it from my dad. I remember it saying he knew I was going through a hard time and that he loved me. As I held this little basket filled with lotion, perfume, and bath bombs, my defenses dropped along with my tears. My thoughts? *Darn it, now I have to be nice to my parents.*

Their show of grace provided me the opportunity to feel as if I didn't have to fight them anymore. And most of the time, I felt as if I had to fight them on everything. The feeling that I had to challenge my parents—I popped out like that. It was just part of my DNA. But this window of kindness led into a heart-to-heart conversation, which then led to a happier and chiller season where Mom and Dad weren't the enemy.

Thoughts to Ponder:

- Have you learned to join your children's dance and enjoy the parenting roller coaster?

- Have you felt frustrated about not being the "ideal" parent? Maybe it's time to accept yourself for who God made you to be and be the best parent you can.

- If you haven't already, consider asking your children the questions at the beginning of this chapter.

Chapter Eight

BREAKING THE CYCLE OF FAMILY DYSFUNCTION

My mother and I have the same name—Lucille. I've always hated my name. As an adult, I finally got the courage to bring up the subject. While on a walk, I asked, "Mom, do you like your name?" She said, "No." I stopped, gave her a blank look, and began to laugh. "Really? Then why in the world did you give it to me?"

"Well, your dad always loved the name."

As parents, we tend to pass on to our kids things we hate about ourselves. How do we not pass down what we don't want to pass down? Is it even possible? If so, how? That's what I asked God, and myself, when I became a parent. And I had a lot of work ahead of me because I had many "issues" I didn't want to pass on, one in particular—my unhealthy relationship with food.

I come from a long line of "professional eaters." Being

Italian, we know how to cook and we know how to eat. Growing up, food and love were synonymous. In my family, if they loved you, they fed you—and they fed you. Actually, even if they just liked you, they fed you. Are you happy? Eat. Are you sad? Eat. Stressed out? Eat. Whatever the problem, food was the cure. For family entertainment, the kids would be gathered around Uncle Pat and watch him eat a big meatball whole as everyone cheered. Eating a lot was like wearing a badge of honor. "Look at her eat! God bless her!" I learned to use food to cope.

Just after getting married, before knowing Christ and before kids, I remember sobbing in the shower and pleading, "God, please help me," to the God I wasn't sure existed. With my tears washing down the drain, I thought if there were a God, He certainly wouldn't accept me. I didn't like the person I had become, and I felt utterly alone and isolated. From the age of sixteen to roughly twenty-two, I battled with bulimia. I felt like I had no control over my life; the disease was winning.

It was my secret until my husband found out. I got professional help and was able to stop. After a couple years in therapy, I became a Christian and handed my life and eating disorder over to God.

> *There is no one holy like the LORD,*
> *indeed, there is no one besides You, nor*
> *is there any rock like our God.*
> 1 SAMUEL 2:2

I've learned to accept myself and accept my wrestling with weight control and body image. However, remnants of the disease have lingered. I love food; I love being around food; I love looking at food; I love talking about food; and I love to watch people eat. Weird, I know. Watching a complete stranger eat a cream puff across the room is like entertainment for me. And I'm not going to tell you how I've wandered through restaurants scoping out the food while waiting for a table. After my kids were born, watching them eat was fun. Even today, it's kind of a family joke. Everyone now knows why Mom is so interested in what you're eating—it's like a food fix for her.

After Monica was born, I vowed I wouldn't pass this dysfunction down to her. I made some rules for myself regarding my daughter. I would not talk about my weight, diets, or the scale in front of her. Nor would I ever criticize her physique or my own, and I would give her compliments about her figure but focusing more on her character.

Passing on a healthy self-image can be almost impossible if we don't possess it ourselves. What is beauty anyway? The world may have us believe a woman is beautiful when she is stacked, racked, ripped, nipped, snipped, plucked, tucked, and liposucked. But true beauty comes from the inside. "Woe to you, scribes and Pharisees, hypocrites! For you are like whitewashed tombs which on the outside appear beautiful, but inside they are full of dead men's bones and all uncleanness" (Matthew 23:27). Real beauty starts on the inside and comes out as we love others and honor God and His Word. "Charm is deceitful and beauty is vain, but a woman who fears the LORD, she shall be praised" (Proverbs 31:30). There's something about a woman who has loved God, loved her family, embraced life with a smile, and focused on being the best version of herself. She seems vibrant as she ages, and even the lines in her face seem soft. Age seems to make her better.

As my daughter grew, I wanted to stay focused on building her inside qualities.

ROLLING WITH THE DONUTS

When Monica was a toddler, I allowed her to eat as much as she wanted, figuring she'd naturally regulate herself. All seemed fine, and I was so proud of myself for being such a progressive mom. Then, during her three-year-old routine checkup, our doctor said these devastating words to me: "Monica is way too chubby for her age and size. She needs to lose weight." My heart skipped a beat. *Oh no, I did it! I passed this terrible dysfunction on to my daughter. How could I do this?! I can't breathe, I can't breathe.*

When I got home, I got on my knees. "God, what do I do?" After praying and talking to my husband, I simmered down and decided to ask a few friends for advice. One friend asked, "Why does it matter what the doctor said? What do you think?" I thought about it, and. . .*she was chubby!*

Mike and I decided to put her on a plan *without her knowing.* We gave her healthy food options and didn't allow her to gorge herself. The words *diet* and *plan* were never used. We never told her she couldn't eat certain foods and never said anything about her being overweight. She still got her share of sweets, just not as frequently. We made extra sure we gave her plenty of fruits and vegetables and did not deprive her at all. When other kids got cookies, she got one too. She just wasn't allowed to eat five. I would talk with her about feeling satisfied in her stomach. When she ate too much or wanted to eat too much, I would tell her, "Honey, it is just not healthy for your little body to have that much food."

In the meantime, I did my best to model a balanced lifestyle by working out on a regular basis and eating healthy—low sugar and lots of fruits and vegetables. A healthy lifestyle is something we can work to pass on. Kids who watched their parents exercise are more likely to exercise as adults. Kids do what they learn. While they are growing up, you control what food comes into your home and what they eat. We all know of young kids who were overweight throughout childhood and entered adulthood obese.

We were committed to raising her with her health in mind. What didn't help was that her younger brother hardly ate. Tim was the kind of kid who'd turn down ice cream if he wasn't hungry, and the tracking he needed was to make sure he ate enough healthy food—leaving me with children on both ends of the scale. Monitoring *more, less, more, less* and keeping the food Tim didn't eat away from Monica were draining. There were days I wanted to give up and just throw a pile of cookies in the middle of the room and let them fend for themselves.

Monica would yell and scream and throw fits when she didn't get her way, such as when she was not allowed to have a second piece of cake or whatever else she wanted. Through the grueling process, I had feared I would one day see her on TV being carried out of her house on a forklift while eating cupcakes...and it would be all my fault. She just did not like the word *no*. Ever. If she wanted it, she demanded it. She'd beg me for food—"Mommy, please, I'm still hungry." But I knew she was not hungry because she had just eaten two helpings of spaghetti and a big salad.

And if she had an audience, that was her cue to try to convince people I was starving her. "Mommy, I am sooo hungry. Please, Mommy, let me eat something." She would have already eaten a big meal and just turned down a healthy snack, but the people watching didn't know that. Sometimes you must suck it up, do what you think is best for your child, and endure the judgmental stares. Once after my cousin stayed with us for a week, she told me, "At first, I thought you were mean when I heard your daughter begging you for food. But then I couldn't believe how much she would eat. You *have to* monitor her."

At times, I was tempted to surrender and let her eat whatever she wanted. I figured, *When she becomes a roly-poly, I'll buy a wagon and pull her around—it'll be fine.*

Finally, I realized this aspect of her personality was really no different from all the other areas of her life. She fought us at every turn, and it felt like she had a calculated master plan to find out if we cared enough to hold our ground. In the end, our toil was worth it—in many areas and with her health. By her next doctor checkup, our once-chubby three-year-old was a healthy weight, and she remained there throughout her childhood. By her teen years, she was regulating herself. *Hallelujah!*

As a teenager, she inspired me in this area. Watching her feel secure with who she was helped me to be more secure with myself. Many times she would say to me, "Mom, you look great!"This was particularly uplifting, especially during a time when she was looking hotter and hotter and I was having hot flashes.

When she became an adult, she shared with me that as a little girl she thought I looked perfect, loved my figure, and had always hoped to look like me when she grew up. I find this a bit odd because I've had difficulties being content with my own body image. I am thankful she never heard me complain about my figure. Knowing this now, I am so glad I never got mad at her for going in my room—without permission—and playing dress-up with my clothes and shoes.

FAMILY WOUNDS

Other wonderful qualities beyond food addiction sailed down through my family as well, like the art of criticism with a specialty in screaming. Wave in some codependency, and I had a lifetime worth of "issues" to work through. I tackled the yelling "talent" as soon as my daughter was born. I made a vow to myself I wouldn't yell at my kids. Yelling at my husband took more work, as chapter 2 already pointed out; but with better communication skills and therapy, I was able to get that under control too.

Wanting to scream always started with a feeling within my heart and gut, a rumbling that felt like an internal explosion. As soon as I felt this coming on, I would stop talking. Period. I figured *if I didn't talk, I couldn't yell.* And then I'd deal with the internal struggle, just me and God. My kids will say if they yelled, I'd say something like "I will not engage you while you are yelling. Once you calm down, we can talk." Today, if someone hollers at me, I will say something like "Please don't yell at me; I don't like it. Can we talk about this and work this through calmly?" What I'm working toward when someone I care about is upset is validating their feelings by saying a version of this: "I understand you're upset or hurt or angry right now. I care about you and am willing to talk with you after the volume goes down." I have such an aversion to being yelled at, I tend to shut down and become silent. Entering into a screaming match doesn't help me solve anything, but it could very well ruin relationships.

As far as the criticism and codependency, I joined a support group to wade through those. Books, podcasts, and therapy have all helped with trauma and shame.

WHERE TO BEGIN?

I can't be a perfect mother, but I can offer my best. It all starts with being honest about yourself with yourself. Admit what areas you struggle with. We tend to operate on automatic pilot and repeat what we know—the good and the bad. We've all got "stuff." No one is exempt. One therapist, who's also a Christian, told me: "There are two types of people in the world: the people who are screwed up and know it, and the people who are screwed up and don't know it."

Getting still, getting alone, and taking time to pray, God will gently show us areas that need attention. Even Jesus did this: "But Jesus Himself would often slip away to the wilderness and pray" (Luke 5:16). And Jesus didn't have any "stuff" to work through. Often, in order to see a problem, we need to step outside of the problem. Stop, spend time with yourself, and spend time with God. Be honest and real with yourself.

Recognizing who we are and intentionally committing ourselves to a different path than what we experienced growing up are so important. Becoming self-aware can be quite challenging but oh so necessary for our emotional health. Dealing with emotional wounds can be very painful—one may be tempted to play the blame game and point fingers at our parents. Part of being self-aware is taking responsibility for ourselves. If there are things from your past you don't want to repeat, take control over whether you will break the cycle.

We all have our own journey. Some of us may need to self-parent, process trauma, and learn to self-regulate. Some may need an ongoing support system. In order to parent our kids in a healthy manner, we first need to learn to self-parent in a healthy way. And for many of us—including myself—this is no easy task. It may mean seeking out a professional. Getting help—in whatever form, whether therapy or through a support group—for you is getting help for your kids.

How do we deal with our kids while we are on our own healing journey? Explaining our struggles to our kids will help them not internalize or carry our struggles unnecessarily. For example, if you catch yourself lashing out at your child, explain it. "I was feeling anxious about being late. I'm sorry I hollered at you. Will you please forgive me?"

"I was feeling frustrated about the dishwasher not working."

"I was feeling agitated over [fill in the blank], and I took it out on you. I'm sorry."

Children understand mistakes and honesty. Keep in mind that what's shared with a seventeen-year-old will be very different than what's shared with a three-year-old.

This was an area where I could have done better. I kept many of my struggles, particularly my "food" struggles, from my kids. I think a big part of it was I had a hard time coming to terms with my "flaws" and thought if I didn't talk about them, somehow they would disappear. My older kids were teenagers before I revealed to them that I had bulimia as a teen and young adult. One day they were talking about eating disorders and how disgusting they were, and I piped in and shared, "Hey, guys, that was me. I had that." Their mouths dropped. I remember feeling like I had just taken off a mask that day, and I realized sharing flawed parts of me was freeing.

Please don't feel discouraged if it seems like you have a lot of "stuff" to work through. Most of us do. It's called being a living and conscious person. Family wounds, trauma, shame, self-regulation, and breaking a cycle of family dysfunction can feel completely overwhelming. Recognizing it first and then handing it over to God are the best steps you can take for changing a generational tide.

God wants us to break free from anything that hinders or binds us. If we recognize those things and hand them over to Him, He offers us freedom. God cares about our affliction and suffering (Isaiah 61:1–3). He cares about every tear and every broken heart. Christ came to set us *free*.

Jesus came to set me free. Jesus came to set *you* free. Surrender to Him, and let Him carry your burdens. There is no promise the waters will always be calm, but He does promise to never leave us. If anything has a strong hold on you, give it to our gracious and loving Father, who is able to deliver us from all our afflictions. He delivered me, and I know He can deliver you.

> *The LORD is near to the brokenhearted and saves those who are crushed in spirit. The afflictions of the righteous are many, but the LORD rescues him from them all.*
> PSALM 34:18–19

— — — — — — — — — — — — —

THOUGHTS FROM MONICA:

I do not have a natural "off switch" when it comes to eating. The ability to know when to stop consuming food was a skill I had to learn. It's so true that I would beg Mom for food as a child. I wanted to eat, but I lacked the understanding between full and satisfied. As a kid, full just meant you were full; it didn't mean you stopped eating. Adding in the fact that Mom said no to some foods from time to time just made me want to fight her on it. It took a lot of training on my mother's part to help me learn what it meant to be healthy and to not overeat. As an adult, I'm really, really thankful she did not give up on this with me.

Once I came into my teen years, I was able to monitor myself. And once I hit adulthood, it finally hit me that

I used food to feel good. Coming from an Italian background, all happy events and occasions involved food—tons of food, usually. Food meant fun, and fun meant happy. I was bored, let's eat. I was sad, let's eat. I was crying, well it's time for a chocolate bar. As a kid, eating made me feel happy, so I went to it whenever I wanted to alter my mood.

But Mom was really excellent at making the focus about health and not about weight. It was about being healthy and consuming the right foods, not about looking skinny. And despite all her hard work to hide her own body image issues and to provide me with a positive physical self-image, I still took notice of her silent struggle and still struggle with all this myself. I knew when she was on a diet. I knew when she was working out more. I knew she was aware of what we all ate. I knew something was up when it came to food and my mom.

Because of clothing sizes, how people look in magazines, peer pressure, and even our own issues, there is no perfect way of putting your child into a bubble and having them come out with the most optimal self-image, no matter what you do. I have come to accept in myself that how I view me and how I gain or lose weight—that is going to be my struggle. But what I don't struggle with is knowing what is healthy and good for my body.

When I started having kids, there was no struggle in knowing what to feed them and how much. Mom had given me the tools. I understood nutrition and exercise and how to read labels and cook healthily. Even with my preschool son now, we're having conversations about how sweets are okay sometimes, not all the time, and how healthy foods make us strong. He gets it.

Mom couldn't shelter me into having a perfect body image. But she did show me that conversations around health are important. I was given a foundation that allowed me to figure out what a healthy relationship with food looked like.

That's the best we can all do with our kids—give them a solid foundation and the right tools so they can build their own healthy lives. And I say that as if it were some easy task. Let's be honest with ourselves, our issues have a wonderful way of bleeding into being a parent. It's one thing for my issues to fall onto my husband—I'm not having to train him how to wipe his "bum bum." A spouse relationship is one of equals not a relationship where I'm trying to help him navigate the world on his own one day. There's so much more at stake with my kids.

Thus, here is my new revelation about parenting: If you want to be a better parent, get into therapy. Why, yes, I have taken my own advice, and it's been *amazing*! It doesn't matter that I had great parents and a decent childhood, I've still got loads of dysfunction I'm working on.

It's easy for me to be angry, which also means I must be aware about keeping my anger in check. My oldest is similar in this way to me. I've recently embraced practices that allow your brain a moment to calm down. What that looks like for a preschooler is having him spread out the fingers of one hand. He then takes the pointer finger of his other hand and traces his hand, starting at the base of his thumb. Each time he traces up, he breathes in; each time he traces down, he exhales, until he's traced his whole hand. It sounds ridiculous, I know, but it works. No joke. And here is how I know it sunk in:

The other day my husband was playing with our son when the little guy began to get worked up over some perceived injustice. Jake was about ready to explode all over Daddy when he stopped and said to himself, "Okay, okay, okay, I need to calm down." He then breathed in and then out, in and then out, in and then on his exhale said to my husband, "I'm fine now." It worked! I got help; I helped my son; and our interactions as a family became far healthier.

Growing up, I watched my parents seek help whether in the form of counsel, therapy, or the Bible. The message was received that physical, spiritual, and emotional health had value. I can only give my kids so much and for however long they will receive it. But while they are receiving, at least I can model the importance of seeking help. They will spend less than a third of their life in my household, where, let's be honest, they're legally required to put up with me. The rest of their life is their own. How they handle their personhood will be their choice. But if I can at least show them the value in seeking God and seeking help, they will have the tools to figure it out on their own.

— — — — — — — — — — — — —

Thoughts to Ponder:

- Is there something from your past that may be hindering your parenting? Maybe it's time to tackle an underlying cause and put it to rest?

- Is there a step you can take today toward a more emotionally healthy lifestyle?
- Maybe your first step is to accept yourself—flaws and all—just the way you are and recognize God loves you just the way you are.

Chapter Nine

ENJOYING THE PARENTING ROLLER COASTER

When you anticipated becoming a parent, did you envision fun and laughter? Before we are parents, we think of parenthood as fun and warm and delightful. It can be all those things, but sometimes the seriousness of life and an impossible kid can get in the way. Parenting is serious business; and if we let the serious side fully take over, we can lose our joy in the thrill of being a parent—the joy of our child's smile, embrace, laugh.

There's a 1989 film titled *Parenthood*. The film depicts the multidimensions and oftentimes complications of parenting. Gil, played by Steve Martin, is a father of three who seems frustrated and disenchanted by the complexity of being a dad. Toward the end of the movie, his wife, Karen, is sewing a costume for a play their daughter, Taylor, will be in that evening. While Karen is talking with Gil, Grandma—who up to this point doesn't seem to be "all there"—enters.

The dialogue that follows is my favorite part of the movie.

Grandma talks about when she was nineteen and Grandpa took her to a roller coaster. Roller coasters have ups and downs and offer a thrilling experience. As Grandma talks Gil gives sarcastic remarks. Grandma didn't care; she kept talking how the ride made her frightened, scared, sick, excited, and thrilled all at the same time. Then she comments that some people didn't like the roller coaster and preferred the merry-go-round. Grandma offered the idea that the merry-go-round was boring and that she preferred the roller coaster. Then, Grandma leaves to go get in the car. Gil continues to poke fun at Grandma, but his wife Karen remarks how brilliant Grandma is, and that she herself LIKES roller coasters. She obviously got the message Grandma was trying to convey while Gil on the other hand makes another snide remark that if Grandma was so brilliant she wouldn't be sitting in their neighbor's car.

Moving ahead to the scene with Taylor's school play underway:

While Taylor's on stage with the other kids, her younger brother, Justin, begins to get upset thinking the other kids are hurting his sister and runs on stage screaming that he's going to save his sister. Once on stage Justin fights with the kids surrounding his sister. Gil is embarrassed and upset at first, but then we hear the sound of a roller coaster, and he begins to "go with the flow" and laughs. It was as if he finally surrendered trying to control and enjoyed the ups and downs of the flow of parenting. He was letting go. . .letting go of control, letting go of what others thought about him, letting go of what others thought about his kids—he let go and came to a point of acceptance.

When we can get to a point of acceptance, we can experience joy. If we are controlled by our fear and anxiety or the need for power, status, and control, it's almost impossible to have joy and see humor in life. I couldn't give my kids a flawless mom, but I could give them one who laughed a lot.

One morning our dog had gotten into the trash in my bathroom, and I hurriedly cleaned it up before heading out. I stopped at the bank and then went to the gym. When I got to the gym, I needed to use the ladies' room and then walked clear across the gym to look for a book I had left the day before. Luckily, I found the book, and I went to start my workout.

First, I did my sit-ups and then moved on to the leg press machine. My feet were planted on the foot plate when I noticed something stuck to the bottom of my shoe. It was sticking out sideways. I quickly grabbed it off my shoe, cupped it in my hand, and hurried outside to a trash can. I opened my hand... *oh no!* It was a panty liner! How did it get there?! How long had it been there?! At that point, I remembered the dog and the trash. That must have been when it got stuck. Now it was time to retrace my steps... *oh no... the bank!* Then the gym, into the bathroom, across the gym to look for my book, sit-ups, and then finally landing on the leg press machine. I broke out in laughter and went back into the gym to finish my workout. Repeating this story to my kids was the highlight of my day.

Laughing at mistakes teaches failure is normal and reminds our kids that Mom is not perfect. My kids got reminded of this regularly, and I learned sharing my what could be embarrassing blunders bolstered our relationship.

LETTING GO

Are you willing to let your children see you as something other than perfect? It's tempting to present a version of ourselves where we "have it all together." However, what lures me more is a pure and solid relationship with my children, one where I can show who I really am without continually having to conceal things out of fear that the "real me" will be revealed. The real you is always better than a facade. The more real you are, the more real your relationships will be.

There was a time when mistakes and blunders caused me to feel shame and embarrassment. *What if someone saw that? What if someone laughed at me?* I would try to do everything just right to avoid these feelings, but of course it was to no avail. I discovered it was much better to laugh at myself and enjoy the craziness. Consider Genesis 21:6, when Sarah was pregnant at the age of ninety. Sarah said, "God has made laughter for me; everyone who hears will laugh with me." Let your kids laugh with you.

When we embrace who we are—quirkiness, mistakes, and blunders—and welcome the funny things or what could be embarrassing things, we are more human to our kids and more approachable. I happen to have ADD, so I'm never short on bloopers. Be willing to notice and laugh when your kids point out funny things you do. Our kids see these things in us and, if they have siblings, are most likely laughing together over the stuff we might try to hide. I know my kids do, and usually right in front of me. If we embrace the funniness in our slipups, we can learn to enjoy slipping. Think about the idea of going through an embarrassing situation, rising above it, and laughing at yourself. Don't you think it's better than feeling devastated or humiliated? The ability to laugh at yourself and passing this gift on to your children creates a positive ripple effect for generations. If you can laugh at yourself, it diminishes the ability to be hurt and makes life more fun.

One of my biggest slips was regarding the Tooth Fairy. No matter how hard I tried, I couldn't seem to remember to put that stinkin' tooth under the pillow in time for the morning reveal. The first morning, Monica woke expecting money but still had a tooth under her pillow. She came to me crying. I felt horrible and told her the Tooth Fairy was running late and she should go look again as I pulled a Houdini and slid money under her pillow. By the time our third child's teeth were falling out, I would tell him to put his tooth under his pillow and sometime within the next two weeks the Tooth Fairy would come. As the kids got older and realized who the unfaithful fairy was, the kids would put the tooth in a baggie and tape it on their door with a sign that read TAKE TOOTH. INSERT MONEY.

When you show your children grace, they are more likely to give grace—to you and others. Over the years, my children learned to have fun with a mom who could be forgetful and easily redirected. One time while in the car with my older two, who were five and six at the time, Monica asked, "Are we late or on time?" I said, "We're early." Together they asked, "What's early?" Check, please. . . But there's more. . .

There was an event at church, and I really wanted to look good and present myself well. I used hair removal cream on my upper lip, got sidetracked, and left the cream on for way too long. By the time I removed the cream, I had burned my lip and had big ugly blisters. I was so tempted to hibernate for a week or so until my mustache blisters cleared up but decided to go anyway, hoping with makeup and lipstick, no one would notice. Nope—everyone noticed. I decided to go with it and revealed, "I had to eat my oatmeal with a baby spoon." I heard, "Lu, next time, why don't you just save yourself the trouble and pour acid on your face!"

It turned out to be more fun than anticipated, and we all had a lot of laughs. Going was definitely better than hibernating.

Laughing at ourselves teaches our kids to laugh at themselves, which builds confidence. When we laugh with our kids, it bolsters our relationships, lowers stress, and creates a bonding experience. Humor is like medicine—it alleviates tension, benefits the heart, heals us, and connects people. Laughter produces endorphins and oxytocin and creates positive memories. Can your kids joke and have fun with you? Not in a mocking or hurtful way but in a fun-loving way? Having fun with someone is being vulnerable with them—it brings down walls and transfers warmth and endearment. One way to open the door to having fun with our kids and create a safe space where they can joke with us is to learn to laugh at ourselves. Children who grow up in a home where humor is fostered are happier and more optimistic and have higher self-esteem. It's easier to weather life's painful circumstances when we set a path for sadness and humor. There is a time for everything—"a time to weep and a time to laugh; a time to mourn and a time to dance" (Ecclesiastes 3:4).

Seeing humor in things started for me as a child. When my

little sister and I were young, we loved to go into the bathroom where my mother kept the dirty clothes hamper and hide in it when we had company. One of us would hide among the dirty clothes quietly, patiently waiting, until someone would use the bathroom. Then we would pop out of the hamper; the commode user would scream; and we'd open the door for the other, who was waiting outside. Oddly, I do not recall anyone ever getting angry. We usually did this to family, and it got everyone roaring with laughter. Why we didn't get in trouble for this is still a mystery.

Having a sense of humor is a learned quality and can be developed and fostered in children. So, laugh at yourself, laugh with your kids, and make space for humor in your everyday situations. Being a parent means there is something to laugh about every day if we look for it.

CREATING HUMOR IN YOUR HOME

How do we set the stage for a humor-filled home?

- Model it, and illustrate that adults are funny. Give your kids something to laugh about.

- Notice your children's humor and bring value to it. See the "funny" and point it out.

- Let your children joke with you, and allow your children to laugh at you and with you.

A good-humored parent is a better parent. We cannot control what happens, but we can control our response to what happens. The relationships we have with our children will be largely determined by the way we respond to them.

Choosing laughter over disgust and humor over anger will build a bond.

One morning my husband and I awoke to the sounds of one of our children banging on the bathroom door and screaming while the child in the bathroom screamed back. My husband's first words to me that day were "Aren't you glad we had kids?" and we laughed. When you're irritated, look for one thing to laugh about. If we look for humor, we find it.

A joyful heart is good medicine,
but a broken spirit dries up the bones.
PROVERBS 17:22

LOOKING IN THE BIBLE

On the note of looking for humor, would you have a little fun with me and can we look for humor in the Bible together? Let's take a bit of a detour, shall we?

In Numbers 22, Balaam was whacking his donkey because the donkey wasn't going where he wanted her to: "Then the LORD opened the mouth of the donkey" (Numbers 22:28), and she *talked*, basically saying, "Stop hitting me! You're nuts."

In Luke 19, Zaccheus, a full-grown man who was short, wealthy, and a chief tax collector, was longing to see Jesus and was hanging out in a tree, probably trying *not* to be noticed. Jesus noticed him and basically said, "Hey Zach, I see you. You're acting a little weird. No wonder people don't like you. Get down from there. I'm inviting Myself over for dinner."

The prophet Elijah, who didn't die but went straight to

heaven via a fiery chariot (2 Kings 2:11), raised a boy from the dead (1 Kings 17:22), called on God and a water-drenched altar exploded into a blaze of fire (1 Kings 18:38), and slew prophets of Baal (1 Kings 18:40) then went on the run (1 Kings 19). Why was he running and who was he afraid of? Elijah, you have raised a boy from the dead, miraculously set an altar on fire, and courageously killed prophets of Baal, so who are you running from? Elijah, catching his breath, says, "Jezebel."

In Acts 12, the apostle Peter was in prison while God's people were praying for him. An angel freed him. Then Peter knocked on the door where his friends were praying.

> Rhoda: Oh, it's you, Peter. I'm so excited you're here.
> Let me tell the others (and she runs off).
> Peter: Are you going to let me in? I'm freezing.
> Rhoda: Peter's here (interrupting the prayer meeting)!
> The Woman who was praying for the longest:
> Yeah, and I'm the King of Egypt!
> Rhoda: No, he's really here!
> The Woman: Geez, Rhoda, enough with your lies!
> Can't you see I'm praying for a miracle here?

Obviously, these are all my versions of the accounts in the Bible. My point is, when we look for humor, we can find it.

KEEPING A JOYFUL HEART

Going with the parenting flow and looking for humor in our daily lives paves the way for the preteen and teenage years. Humor can lighten stressful and tense situations.

As Monica grew into the preteen years, her face told me what I was probably going to be dealing with. One day she asked me, "How do you know I have an attitude, and how do you know what I'm about to say?"

"Well, honey, come with me." I took her in the bathroom and had her face the mirror. She had her arms folded and had a look on her face that said, "I'm taking on the world. You just try to stop me. And by the way, I'm not happy about your interference one bit!"

I said, "Look."

She replied, "What?"

"Look at your face in the mirror. That's what I see. That's the attitude."

She looked, saw the "face," kept the frown for a couple of seconds, and then we both broke into laughter.

One day, as we hurried to make our dentist appointment, Monica and I were having a day filled with more conflict than usual. Monica was a teenager at the time. When we left our doctor's office, we had to exit down a flight of stairs, and Monica said, "I was going to tell you to go first so I could push you down the stairs." We laughed, and it broke the ice.

RIDING THE ROLLER COASTER WITH A TEENAGER

You may be on the up-and-down ride with a teenager now or you'll be on it later—either way, it's never too soon to buckle up and throw your hands up (to God). Do you remember your teen years? Do you remember how difficult they were? A teenager is not an adult and yet not a child either. They don't seem to fit in the world yet. Everything is changing, from their bodies to their emotions. Their brains go on overdrive, pumping hormones into their bodies to get them ready for adulthood. Between surging hormones, mean-girl politics, social media comparisons, and online gaming, your kids are trying to find their way. Those same hormones drive their increasing sexual awareness and often moodiness and aggressiveness. But these hormonal changes often come before your adolescent has the reasoning capacity to handle it. In this season, what you do to be the stable ground for your teen will be crucial. This is the time to dig deep with care, sensitivity, and understanding. Establish a fun-loving and forgiving environment to guide you into the beginning of your new relationship with your soon-to-be-adult child.

As children get older and feel the need to stake out their own territory, they may sometimes push you away as a way of gaining independence. It's healthy as they grow and mature to learn they can stand on their own *without* Mom. When this happens, don't be alarmed or get upset. They run back as fast as they push you away. Do your best to refrain from getting angry, and try not to react to their reactions. (I know it's hard.)

When Joseph wanted to walk home from school in the sixth grade, I would walk partway to meet him. If he was with his friends, he would act like he didn't know me—and I'd play along. It was quite funny. I would wait until his friends were gone and then embrace him, and we'd walk the rest of the way home together. There was no need for offense; he was exercising his individuality, independence, and separateness.

Sometimes we need to give our children space to enable

them to grow and mature. Sometimes we need to get out of the way and let God deal with them. When your children need space, don't take it personally. It's part of growing up.

One day while picking Tim up from high school, Joey and I walked on campus and waited for him. I could see the panic on Tim's face when he saw us. Mumbling under his breath, "Mom, what are you doing here?! Are you trying to embarrass me?"

"Just walk," I said quietly. "No one needs to know we are here for you. The car is on the street."

Once in the car, Tim said, "Mom, *never* get out of the car! Why did you do that?"

"What? I wasn't trying to do anything. What's the big deal?"

"Never get out of the car."

"Why?"

"Do you see any other parents getting out of their cars? Never get out of the car."

"What if I looked like a hot model? Would it be okay to get out of the car then?"

"No! It has nothing to do with how you look. The other parents don't get out of their cars. Never get out of the car. That was so embarrassing! It was bad enough to have *you* there and then Joey runs up to me."

"Well, now I know how to embarrass you. Next time maybe I'll bring Dad."

Monica was different; she didn't mind if I went on campus. Each child has their own special dance, and it's our job to guide, love, and embrace who they are. . .like God does with us. Each child goes through the teen years differently.

The harder the season for your child, the more engaged you need to be. Many believe the teen years need less engagement; however, I propose this is when you need to be around your children the most. One mom of a teenage girl told me, "I just can't stand to be around her right now." I know these years can feel like you're giving and giving, and you might be tempted to throw up the white flag and retreat, but stay engaged; they can be the most fun and rewarding years too.

The snottier and more abrasive they are, the more time they need. If they are acting out, there is probably something going on, and you need to find out what it is. If you take time to be with your teens and listen, really listen, you can encourage, support, and guide them toward wise decisions. Spending time with your teens also communicates importance and says "What you are going through matters to me." You'll be surprised what a stop for breakfast on the way to school can accomplish. Stay engaged even though it may feel like they want you to check out.

Our teens need to feel safe and not afraid to come to us when things go wrong. I can remember the crippling feeling as I threw dirt over the side of my dad's new car to hide the scratch I had made. After driving home, I fessed up because the anxiety overwhelmed me. He took it better than expected, but thinking back on it now, I can still tap into the panic I felt.

It's important to let your teens know they are more important to you than material things or how others perceive you. Pastor Andy Stanley grew up as a pastor's kid (his father is Dr. Charles Stanley), and he tells the following story from when he was a teenager: He and his friend Louie Giglio would attend Sunday school and then walk to a restaurant, order some food, find an empty eating room, and change the channel to their church's worship service, which was broadcast live. One Sunday, while he was driving home from church with his father, his father said, "Andy, Evelyn told me that someone told her that they saw you and Louie leaving the church, leaving the church property, right after Sunday school." Then he paused and said, "And Andy, do you know what I told her?" Andy said, "No, sir." His father said, "I told her, you tell your friend to raise her kids and I'll raise mine." Andy said, "In that moment, I felt drawn in rather than pushed away . . .I knew I was more important to my dad than his public reputation. He put me first. The next Sunday, Louie and I were on the second row. A defining moment is better than a teachable moment." *

If you focus on the relationship and building mutual trust, the teen years do not have to be as bad as the nightmare stories you've heard. For instance, our children never had a curfew. They let us know where they were, what time they'd be home, and whom they'd be with. As an adult, Monica later told me sometimes she wouldn't go out in order to avoid all our questions. She knew if she couldn't answer who, where, and what, we wouldn't be comfortable, and she respected that.

WOE IS ME; I HAVE A TEENAGER

Some friends—a delightful couple—asked me for guidance in dealing with what they deemed an unruly teen. They invited me for dinner. As we sat down for our meal, it was just me and them. Their sixteen-year-old daughter would arrive later after her volleyball practice. I heard story after story of how difficult this child was. Anything I said was met with another story of their woes and angst. I listened and prayed for an opportunity to give insight that might help. The opportunity didn't arise, though, because they just wanted to vent their woes of having a teenager.

When the child arrived home, all seemed clear to me. She was not greeted warmly nor given validation to join and be part of our conversation. Instead, this teenager was met with "Did you finish the chores I left you to do?" "Why didn't you do your homework?" "Why were you so late?" Her parents not only neglected to show delight in her, but their body language was that of disapproval. Their tone was that of disgust.

These parents genuinely cared about and loved their daughter. They just didn't know how to communicate that love to her. I had the opportunity to spend time with this teenager the week prior, and she had told me she didn't feel understood or supported by her parents.

How can parents turn this around? Let's play out the above scene in a better way. When the teen arrived home, a sincere greeting with delight coupled with hugs and enthusiasm would have shown love and approval. Then, "How was your day?" or "How was practice?" would have offered interest. They should have followed with an invitation to join us and be included, giving their daughter a place to belong and interact and feel wanted.

Include your children in discussions, and give their views validation; this shows they have value. Homework and chores can be addressed later, not in front of company, not when they first get home, and not communicated with disapproval.

HANDS UP AND LAUGH

Teenagers want to be heard and understood. Just like us, they desire to feel included, supported, and valued. Going back to "the golden rule" mentioned in chapter 6, treat them the way you would want to be treated in good times and bad. They want you to bridge the gap between their world and yours even when they are pushing you away. Personally, I have a struggle with feeling wanted. It's a wound I've carried for many years. It's like I'm a little girl asking for someone to "choose me." Your teens want to feel wanted; it's like they are saying to you and the world, "Choose me." It's our job as parents to be a loving and supportive guide as they find their way.

Keep looking up, you brave and wonderful and courageous mom. God made you with the ability to cry and laugh. A humor-filled home sets a foundation for love and laughter. Make space in your schedule to have fun with your kids. Spend time with them when there is no agenda attached. Pause from being the "parent" and enjoy them. Everything you do matters. Every talk. Every ice cream cone. Every walk. Every burger. Every car ride. Every dinner. Every hug. Every "I love you." Every laugh.

— — — — — — — — — — — — — —

THOUGHTS FROM MONICA:

I wasn't going to actually push her down the stairs—I just want to clarify that first and foremost. But reading that story again, it made me laugh so hard. You may be thinking, "What a horrible thing to say to your mother." And yes, it was; but I knew by saying it, I could get my mom to crack. If you could get Mom to laugh, you could break any tension. She was and still is always willing to laugh at herself. All three of us love poking fun at her. It was clear early on that humor was an appropriate form of communication and way to show love. And this has often befuddled onlookers.

My mom was in the room when I was giving birth to my first. And let me tell you, it was a long process. I was in the middle of a three-hour pushing session on the verge of an emergency C-section because this child decided to take his time. I had my husband, a midwife, and three nurses urging me along. Mom started getting a little teary-eyed. I jokingly shouted over to her, "Hold it together, woman!" Now, in Mom and Monica language, that meant, "It's okay. I'm fine. This is all going to be fine." Mom knew that, but the midwife did not. The midwife then snapped at me, "Your mother can cry if she wants to!" I wanted to look at her and go, "You don't understand. This is how we talk." But considering I was in the middle of a contraction, about to shove a whole person out of my body, I decided to let it go. Needless to say, baby arrived safely, and Mom was not offended.

One of my earliest memories, around four or five, was the family sitting around the dinner table laughing. At the time, I was in a ballet class, and while at dinner, my dad would ask if I had learned certain moves—moves like the dying frog. Then I would ask, "What's the dying frog?" Dad would jump out of his chair, hop twice on all fours, and then roll over onto his back with his hands and legs in the air. My brother and I were laughing so hard that our stomachs hurt. I looked over, and Mom was laughing too.

Life, even from an early age, was marked by humor. No matter the fight or awful circumstance, it would eventually lead to laughing. It taught me I could laugh at myself. It taught me to find humor in those awkward situations when one is out of control. It taught me my parents didn't think themselves above us kids. It taught me that a little change in perspective can lift the soul. And ultimately, humor brought us together more as a family.

It was certainly helpful in dealing with Mom's ADD. Mind you, we all didn't formally know Mom had ADD until we were adults, but as kids, we knew there was something off with Mom's attention span. If you have a family member with this, you understand it can be stressful at times to keep up, follow them in conversation, or be offended as to why they can't stay focused on you. Basically, Mom's ADD was the sixth family member. But as you can see, we all learned to joke about it.

Picture this: My brothers and my mom and I are in the middle of a movie. Mom asks us to pause it for a bathroom break. Yeah, sure, no problem. It's paused; she runs off. We're left there sitting and waiting. . .and waiting. . .and waiting. A solid ten minutes go by. The three of us are all speculating as to what happened to her. I head off down the hallway, into her bedroom, and proceed into her bathroom to find her on her knees with a scrub brush in hand, cleaning the toilet. Flabbergasted, I ask her, "What are you doing?! We're in the middle of a movie!" She's jolted back to reality, and I can tell by her response, she entirely lost track of time. She replies, "Oh right, sorry, I'll be right out. I got in here, and I remembered I needed to clean the bathroom." I go back to the living room, where the three of us are completely busting up over the fact that she forgot we were all hanging out. I can promise you, we didn't let her forget her faux pas for the rest of the day. . .or ever.

But Mom was never offended when we brought to her attention that she had spaced out, was talking too fast to follow, or wasn't paying attention when one of us was talking. We learned from an early age it was fine to point it out— she wasn't going to be angry with us or embarrassed. We all learned to accept it. And Mom also gave us permission to laugh with her about these odd moments. Laughter helped maintain our relationship.

Both Mom and Dad were big on maintaining our relationships with them, especially during the teen years. Truthfully, they were a bit pushy at times when it came to what we were thinking and feeling, which as a teen was incredibly annoying. And at other times, I would be waiting for her to ask me just enough questions so I would have an excuse to talk about what I was dealing with at the time. And I always knew as a teen, I didn't have to be afraid of going to them when things went wrong. One time, it went really wrong.

In the summer before I went into high school, I had been sewing in my room. I was patching a rip in one of my shirts, when I somehow lost track of a needle in the carpet. I searched a little bit but couldn't seem to find it. I just decided to let it go. I figured the vacuum would get it. It did not.

A few days later, I walked into my room barefoot, about to hop into my bed, when I heard a popping sound and felt a sharp pain in my left foot. I jumped into bed, brought my foot to my face, and I found a little puncture hole. I was hoping it was only a prick, so I went looking in the carpet for the needle. I found it. But I only found half of a one-inch needle, and then I was fairly certain there was half a metal piece in my foot. I panicked. I lost my mind with worry while squeezing the entry point on my foot, hoping it will pop out like a zit. Terrified, defeated, and heart pounding, usually I would have gone to Mom with something like this, but she was out of town, so I had to go confess to my dad what an idiot I was.

I walked into his office on the verge of tears, and with a shaky voice, I told him I stepped on a needle and it broke off in my foot. He said, "Okay, let's go." He packed me up in the car and took me straight to the foot doctor. On the car ride there, I told him the whole story and how stupid I felt for not forcing myself to find the needle. He just listened. At the doctor's office, Dad was super chill, joking with me, joking with the doctor. I wasn't sure if I was more nervous about the needle or the impending lecture from Dad about being more careful. Turned out the doctor had to cut open my foot and go searching for the needle. He told us this could take five minutes or five hours. It luckily turned out to be only ten minutes. My foot was stitched and wrapped, and I was on crutches until it healed.

Never once did my dad yell or chastise. He didn't even get mad. And what I mostly remember on that day was how much of a concerned parent he was. I could tell he was worried about me. My actions weren't met with a scolding; they were met with kindness and concern. That day taught me I could go to Dad whenever I was in trouble, even if the trouble was my fault. Later we laughed about it.

Laughter was a huge part of my childhood, and it's

something I strive for with my kids—the ability to laugh at the everyday disasters. And when you're raising kids, there are so many imperfect moments.

I'm a planner. I love planning outings and trips for us to do as a family. I'll create this wonderful fantasy in my head on how the day is going to proceed, and would you believe it, it never turns out how I imagined.

Take my son's fourth birthday. His 2020 birthday was smack in the middle of the coronavirus pandemic. Fortunately, weeks prior, the Los Angeles Zoo reopened. Only a limited number of guests were allowed entrance per day, but you had to make sure to reserve the tickets ahead of time. As soon as the tickets were released online, I was up early that morning booking them because I wanted to ensure my baby would have a spectacular day at the zoo for his birthday.

When his big day arrived, everything was going perfectly. We were there on time, I was chill and hardly neurotic, no one was fighting, and we even brought Grandma along. We got into the park and were having a great time. I was really pumped because getting to breathe fresh air after quarantine was an absolute high. Smiling, I looked at my son and asked him if he was having fun. Jake looked at me and replied, "I'm bored. Can we go to Grandma's house?"

My husband, my mother, and I buckled over in laughter. What four-year-old is not into the zoo?! My son, apparently. We convinced him to hang in there a bit longer, considering we'd been in the park only twenty minutes. Luckily, Daddy was pulling him and his sister around in a red wagon the whole time, so it made Jake's experience bearable.

The day continued with my preschooler acting like an

unenthused teenager. We stopped at the giraffes, which were literally feet away from us. "Jake! Look! It's a giraffe!" He looked up and said, "Oh. . .next." We laughed some more.

He wanted to get out and walk, great. Then we were treading along, but Jake's poor legs seemed to give out, and he decided to park it in the middle of the walkway and announce that he was very tired. And so, we laughed some more.

After hours in the park, we made it back to our car, and we were on the road again. I asked Jake what his favorite part of the zoo was, and his answer? "The restaurant." The big highlight of his day was when we stopped for an overpriced peanut butter and jelly sandwich at Gorilla George's Café. You guessed it, we laughed even more.

The fantasy of my son being so appreciative of me and this wonderful outing did not come to fruition, but we had a great day. Even Jake had a great time. He spent time with his favorite people, hardly had to walk anywhere (thanks to his wagon-pulling dad), and finally got to eat out for the first time after quarantine—of course the restaurant was the best part! I could have been offended. I could have been hurt. But fun and funny is where you find it. And when you have kids, funny is everywhere.

Through my childhood years, there was no human being funnier than Daddy. That man had the joke thing down. In my little eyes, Mom was much more serious and could not compare when it came to Dad in this arena. But as I approached my teen years, I had this striking epiphany hit me one day, and I have never forgotten it since. I had just gone on a trip with my mom when we were getting out of the car, headed into the house. She said something that was witty and amusing. I found myself laughing. . .like *really* laughing. I still to this day have no idea what she said that was so amusing, but I do remember saying this: "Mom, you're like really funny. You're way funnier than Dad."

Her response: "I know."

— — — — — — — — — — — — —

Thoughts to Ponder:

- How about you? Do you have some funny stories you can share with your children?

- When was the last time you laughed with your kids?

- Do you need to add more balance to your life by adding a little fun?

*Andy Stanley, Northpoint Church, *Parenting in the 21ˢᵗ Century*, October 2020.

Chapter Ten

LOVE, SEX, AND BROKEN HEARTS

After Monica's first brother was born, Grandma Millie sent a gift of a life-size baby boy, and it came with the *whole* package—genitals and all. My husband put a diaper on the doll and fastened it tightly with duct tape. Monica was still in diapers herself, and we tried to hide the male anatomy with duct tape. Why are we so afraid of our kids' sexuality? The idea that our children are sexual beings can be quite uncomfortable for a parent, and yet, if we don't come to terms with this prickly fact, we will do our kids a disservice. We do everything we can to keep them from sexual activity, and then after they marry, we ask for grandchildren sooner than later. If we want what's best for our children, a healthy sex life—which is certainly one of God's greatest gifts—can definitely be on the list, but how can we prepare them for this?

God created sexual intimacy, and He created our children

as sexual beings. We don't need to be afraid of this. My little grandson, who's four right now, loves to run around naked. He'll be in the bathroom preparing for a bath, and if he sees an opening, he will plow through the door and start running and screaming, "Naked boy... Penis, penis, penis..." Here's the tricky part to this scene: If handled poorly, it could leave him with "issues" surrounding his anatomy and personal identity. Wisely, my daughter simply says, "Back in the bathroom. It's bath time." I don't respond at all except to laugh when he's not looking.

I remember my mother saying to me, "You're boy crazy! I better not catch you kissing any boys!" Question: Is it wrong to be boy crazy? I mean, boys are pretty cool. I've always liked boys, and now I'm crazy about my husband. I understand my mother's fears, but being boy crazy or girl crazy is kind of normal, considering the way God designed us. I thought this was a "bad" part of me, and I hid anything boy related from my mom. I concluded talking to her would mean she'd be disappointed in me or possibly reject me. Risking rejection or condemnation far outweighed taking the chance and going to her with my questions or "boy problems."

Raising a child today with God's standard of purity is a difficult task. The world we live in is teaching our children everything but God's standard. All they have to do is be on the internet, watch TV, go to the movies, or attend school to get the world's view about relationships.

Flee sexual immorality. Every other sin that a person commits is outside the body, but the sexually

immoral person sins against his own body. Or do
you not know that your body is a temple of
the Holy Spirit within you, whom you have
from God, and that you are not your own?
1 CORINTHIANS 6:18–19

An important aspect to this is to communicate to our children that they have the power to use the word *no*. From the time they learn verbal skills, the word *no* is crucial. When you respect your child's *no*, it shows you respect them. Give choices as well as opportunities to use the word *no* and where you listen and respond. This teaches children they have domain over their own personhood and body. Even something as simple as "May I have one of your french fries?" when met with a no, should be respected. It teaches that *no* has power and can be used. This also helps a child say no to themselves and to have self-respect. We also need to teach our children to respect when others use the word *no*.

Guiding our children requires talking about tough and emotionally charged topics like sex and relationships without overreacting. Make talking about relationships, dating, and sex commonplace in your home. Create an environment where it is as easy to talk about the "tough stuff" as it is to talk about sports or the weather. If they know they can talk with you about relationships without embarrassment, they will.

Listening without reacting is a crucial practice if you want to hear whom they are trying to get attention from. This is especially true when they reach the teen years. Everything inside you will be screaming *No!* but on the outside be calm, cool, and collected. If you react with condemnation, they will be less likely to share what is happening with their boy/girl interactions.

God made us with desires for sexual intimacy, and when we deny the truth of this with our kids, it shows we really don't understand what they are going through. The key to open communication is to partner with them and seek to grasp their world by listening more and talking less. Ask more questions instead of offering all the answers. Listen, listen, listen, and remember that the Gospel message screams grace.

I have worked with many teenagers over the years, and a common dilemma I hear expressed is fear their parents will overreact or will hand down consequences they don't think they can endure, if they share various struggles. As a result, many have dealt with suicidal thoughts, depression, drug use, and sexual activity on their own, feeling isolated and alone. One teenager told me all she had to do was mention a boy's name, and her parents would "freak out." Therefore, instead of talking to her parents about boys, she would navigate her relationships on her own and lie about texting and interactions with boys. She even had secret boyfriends. I found this to be common among the teens in the small group I led.

Some teens have reached out to me dealing with same-sex feelings. Usually they are petrified to share "experimenting" or "feelings" they've had with their parents. These children feel extreme isolation and despair and are very confused. After listening to their stories, I'd convey God loves them no matter what they've ever done or will ever do. Then I'd encourage them to love and seek God and to talk with their parents.

HANDLING MESS-UPS

One of my husband's famous lines with all three of our kids was "I am giving you grace because God gives me grace." This basically meant they were getting a free pass. It also communicated he recognized how we all make mistakes, and grace is abundant.

How does God treat us when we fall short? When we take our messes to God, He wraps His arms around us and says, "It's okay. We will get through this together." When our children mess up, they need to know we will walk through whatever the mistake is with them and we will stand by their side. They need to know our love for them has not changed at all. They need to know we forgive them and accept them no matter what they may have done and no matter what they might do in the future. They need to know we are still proud of them. We all yearn for parents in our lives who love and support us no matter what—someone to be a picture of God's love for us that says no matter what you do, no matter what you say, even if I disagree with you, I still love and support you. When we love and fully accept our children through their junk, we are taking them straight to the heart of God.

LOVE AND SUPPORT

During my summer break from junior high school, I was on my "cool" ten-speed bike headed home when I was struck by a pickup truck while crossing an intersection. Witnesses said I flew quite a distance into the air. After hitting the pavement, surprisingly, I stood to my feet and tried to get back on my bike. All I wanted to do was go home, but my bike was smashed. The nice elderly gentleman—who seemed genuinely remorseful—took my bike, put it in the back of his truck, and drove me home. We went to the front door and rang the bell. As my mother answered the door, I began to cry, "Mom, I got hit by a car." I hadn't cried up until that point; oddly, my concern had been for the elderly gentleman. But after seeing Mom, it hit me what had happened, and the flood of emotion poured out. Then my mother put me in her arms. I was finally safe.

There is nothing like being in the arms of a loving parent—safe, secure, free from harm. Human touch—there is no substitute. Loving touch can say "You're okay; I love you; I accept you; you matter; you have value." As you know, children are born needing love and warmth, and if it's absent, it leaves one searching for a substitute. Lavish your kids with hugs throughout the day and couple them with the words "I love you," even through the awkward teen years. It sounds simple, but with the busyness of parenting, we can forget this simple and powerful validation.

Displays of appropriate affection can become a habit. It only takes two seconds to squeeze his arm, touch her cheek, give a kiss on the forehead, or to give a warm embrace; yet, these affirming actions will have lasting effects that will carry into adulthood. Can a parent really show too much love and approval to their children? Sometimes it takes regular intentionality to hug our kids each day.

If possible, encourage a relationship with the other parent whether or not you are still married to them. Monica frequently spent one-on-one time with her dad. Even recently, when I was out of town, I called home and Mike told me

Monica was over for the day—all by herself.

Mike and I did our best to be appropriately affectionate with each of our kids. I had ignorantly thought if she had a close relationship with her dad and we gave her lots of affection, she wouldn't be overly interested in boys while she was growing up. Oh silly, silly, mom! Of course, that wasn't the case.

BOYS

Monica became interested in boys in kindergarten. How would I keep her from being "physical" with these boys she was so crazy about? Adorable, freckled, chubby-cheeked Tyler, the boy who sat in the little chair next to her in kindergarten, became her boyfriend—and the whole class knew they were an item.

I used her "relationship" with Tyler to talk with her about boys. As she went into the second grade and was way more mature, she had two boyfriends. If that wasn't enough to give a mother reason for concern, one day I discovered something during lunchtime at school. Monica was sitting with her friends on the playground. . .and her shirt was tied up and her shorts were rolled up. This belly-showing second-grader in short shorts was not the little girl who had gotten out of my car in the morning! Now I knew why we switched from dresses to shorts and button-down shirts. Pressing through my shock and awe, I asked her friends, "So ladies, does Monica tie up her shirt often?"

The answer I got was "Oh yes, Mrs. Williams, every day." *Clearly, I was the last invited to the party.*

That's it, I'm out. Mike and I decided this was a talk for Dad. He quickly got to the bottom of why she was tying up and rolling up her clothes. It was for the boys! At a very young age, she knew what attracted the opposite sex. It wasn't cookies, it wasn't chatter, and it wasn't cute little dresses below the knees. It was nice-looking legs and belly buttons! Hers! It was wise of me to hand this one to Mike because he was gentle and understanding. After her talk with Dad, she stopped tying stuff up, and I know this because I showed up at the school randomly to check.

Let's recap here: she's in second grade, has two boyfriends, and loves the attention she gets from boys. *Who is this child's mom?*

Then I got the question, "Mom, am I allowed to kiss boys?" *Are you kidding me right now?*

I said, "Yup."

"I am?!" she said with astonishment.

Given her personality, I knew if I had said no, it would have been her goal to explore the possibilities. I did not want to make kissing seem off-limits, because then she would have wanted to push the limits. Instead, I talked with her about why it wasn't a good idea. I told her, "Honey, you could kiss a boy, and I would never know. So, telling you that you can't seems silly to me. I am not going to be with you all the time, and you are going to have to make good decisions on your own, and I trust that you will."

When Monica was in the third grade while our family was walking through a restaurant parking lot, she announced, "Mom, when I see boys, I want to hug them and kiss them." *Maybe it's time to send her to an all-girls boarding school?*

My reply was "I know! I felt the same way. That's why I married your dad."

Kind of an odd response, I know, but again, considering her temperament, if I gave the impression it was some kind of "forbidden fruit," she'd want to hug and kiss all the more. It was more important than ever that I check in with her, talk, and listen, listen, listen.

Some subjects I had to tackle before I wanted to. Like the day she came home and declared, "Tyler is cheating on me! I saw him with that Chelsea again!" We also had talks that started with her declaration of "I don't know if I like Tyler or Daniel more." All the while my underlying objective was to emphasize and reinforce as subtly as possible that she did not *need* a boyfriend. My advice remained the same: just be friends with the boys. Nonetheless, I listened to those long conversations. And more importantly, I didn't leak any condemnation or judgment but made it a fun topic of discussion between us girls. Then behind a closed door, I'd get on my knees and, later, lament to my husband about my concerns. But to Monica, this subject was just fun.

Daniel ended up moving away, and she and Tyler broke up. She was in the third grade and finally single. I talked with her about what it felt like to be someone's ex-girlfriend. Fortunately, she did not like the way it felt, and she especially didn't like how the other children talked about it. This opened a door of opportunity to talk about the ramifications of having a boyfriend, breaking up, and waiting until marriage for intimacy.

Then, pleasantly and unexpectantly, we had a long dry spell from boys. Hallelujah! Our conversations switched from "What do I do about my boyfriends?" to "Why don't I have a boyfriend?" which was fine with me.

When Monica was fifteen—on Valentine's Day—her dad gave her a gold ring with a heart. The ring was a symbol. Mike told her it was his job to guard her heart until she got married, but once she did, she was to give the ring back to him, signifying giving her heart to her husband.

THEN, ALONG CAME TROUBLE IN THE NAME OF LOVE

Enter...we're going to call him John. Monica was only sixteen, and *he* was twenty. Yes, twenty! Now we really had a situation. John worked at our church. Mike had befriended him, like a father figure, and we all grew to love him. In addition, Mike did premarital counseling for John and his girlfriend.

When John broke up with his girlfriend, he became interested in Monica. By this time, he was close to our family and was spending a lot of time with us. Thinking about this now, we were a bit dense, considering the age of our daughter, but we sincerely had not seen it coming. At first it seemed like they had a brother/sister friendship, and then it became apparent they had a "thing" for each other.

I suppose at this point we could have banned him from our family, but it didn't seem right or wise. Suddenly, the greatest fear in my life became the possibility of my sixteen-year-old daughter running off with this *man*—who, by the way, had his own job, his own car, and his own apartment. *Dear God, please help me.* Doing something that made him even more appealing, like restricting her from seeing him, didn't seem like a viable option.

Remember: Monica had a "just-dare-me-not-to-do-it"

demeanor, and we were not about to make this a "You-and-Me-Against-the-World" love story, catapulting them into the sunset together. The person most upset, however, was Mike. He let Monica and John know he was not at all happy with their interest in each other. John officially became her un-boyfriend. "Un" because we would not allow them to date until Monica turned eighteen, figuring if he could wait until then, he'd earned himself a date.

You may be wondering how we kept them from dating. We kept ourselves very available and stayed close. They could be together as long as Mike and I were nearby. Mike was very clear on his expectations—feel free to read between the lines here. In addition, Tony, our Italian friend who was more like family—think 1990 *Goodfellas* movie—pulled John aside one day, put his arm around his shoulder, and said, "If you disrespect Monica in anyway, I will find you, and I will hurt you."

John's response was "Yes, sir."

When Monica found out, she said, "I love Uncle Tony." (She'd called him uncle since she could talk.)

My approach was a bit different. I figured if he became extremely familiar, she would lose interest, and I allowed him to hang out with us as much as he wanted to. I also made sure I spent a lot of time talking with Monica about her feelings. Psalm 55:17 became my daily prayer: "Evening and morning and at noon, I will complain and moan, and He will hear my voice."

Days turned into weeks, which turned into months, and after a year he was still around. A year, and he was twenty-one! And Monica turned seventeen. So much for my thinking she would lose interest. *Way to go, Mom.* Mike became increasingly unhappy with their closeness, and Monica attempted many times to break up with her "un" boyfriend. Somehow John always managed to work his way back into her life. They were spending more and more time together. He was at our house almost every night and always spent every weekend with us—*the whole weekend.*

Suddenly, it hit me. John was smothering her. This "un" boyfriend relationship was getting out of hand. I called Mike and expressed my concerns. He was relieved that we were finally on the same page. I did what any normal mother would do. I sat down and wrote the "Monica & John Rules." And here they are in their original form for your amusement.

MONICA & JOHN RULES

1. There must be space between you on the couch. No sharing blankets or touching of any kind.
2. An adult must be in the room at all times.
3. John leaves at 9:00 p.m. on all school nights. Other nights are up to parental discretion.
4. You can choose one time to be together on the weekends. Friday night, Saturday day, Saturday night, or Sunday after church. Once that time is up, don't ask for more time. More time may be granted by "the King" [i.e., Mike] at his discretion. Asking for more time could result in the removal of the following weekend.
5. No driving alone together. All driving together is by permission only.
6. Mom and Dad leave, John leaves.

7. Hello and goodbye hugs are okay as long as they do not get out of hand.
8. Clothes must remain on at all times. Removal of any clothing will result in an automatic suspension.
9. Lips cannot touch any part of the other person's body.
10. No holding hands unless someone is in danger of falling off a bridge.
11. All rules are subject to change at any time by a word of "the King."

When Monica got home from school that day, I presented her with the rules. *Explosion! Surprise, surprise.* To say she was extremely angry would be putting it mildly. She wouldn't talk to me but instead slammed the door behind her as she went into her room.

Was my seventeen-year-old going to run off with this man using her bedroom window as her getaway? I was anxiously questioning if I had totally blown it. Panicked and paralyzed, I prayed and waited.

Finally, after a grueling hour of waiting, Monica emerged from her room. She wanted to talk, and we went into my room and sat down. I listened intently. Monica talked about the intense inner conflict she felt, wanting to end the relationship but not feeling strong enough to actually follow through. She revealed that John had indeed tried some "funny business," which she rejected. (Lucky for him we never told Uncle Tony!) Bottom line, she decided she would rather break it off with him than follow the new written rules. *She* decided to break things off.

Hours later, when Mike arrived home, she and I were

both crying and sitting in the dark. After Monica told her dad about her decision, Mike suggested she pray first and wait until the next day to talk with John. She did, and that was the last scene of our scary romance saga—and her first heartbreak.

After Monica was an adult, she dated some men, became friends with most, and ended up falling in love with one of her closest friends, Kyle.

Years later, as her wedding day approached, Mike started murmuring about how she needed to return the ring he had given her. But Monica had something else planned. On her wedding day, when they announced it was time for the father/daughter dance, Monica requested the microphone. She said, "Dad, I know you've been wondering what I did with the promise ring. I'm actually wearing it today. When you gave it to me, you said you wanted it back after I found the man I was going to marry. But I was wondering if I could keep it so that I can keep this little piece of you with me." If there was a dry eye in the room, I couldn't see it due to the floods of tears streaming down my face. I've never seen so many grown men crying. Monica always had a sweet relationship with her father.

Going back to when she was about to turn seventeen, I asked her what she wanted to do for her birthday. Her response was beautiful: "I want to go out with Dad." She knew I would do my best to do whatever she wanted, and all she asked for was a date with her dad. This surprised me because this was during her "un" boyfriend interlude.

I wanted to make this evening very special for her since she asked for something so simple—not a party, no expensive trip to Tahiti, no fancy material object, just a date with her dad. I began saving money each week until I had enough to surprise her with a limousine. When she and her dad were ready to leave for the evening, there was a limo waiting with flowers and a red carpet. When given the choice to do whatever she wanted, what would make a teenage girl choose to celebrate her seventeenth birthday with her dad? I'll leave this question for Monica.

— — — — — — — — — — — —

THOUGHTS FROM MONICA:

This has been the most challenging chapter for me—diving back into this time as a teenager, navigating the dating scene for the first time in my life. It's not a mental headspace I'm excited to explore yet again. But also, it was the first time I really began to experience a sense of depression. Prior to this, I had sad days, but after the breakup, it became something more. It turned into days where I didn't want to go to school; I didn't want to be around people; I didn't want to leave my room. This relationship with John—the nature of it, the age difference, the not being technically allowed to date him—I didn't have the tools or the maturity to navigate a relationship with someone who was an adult.

Despite my being mature, I still hadn't arrived at the maturity level to handle a serious dating relationship. Through this whole period, I isolated myself from family and friends. And I was lonely. Sure, I had a boyfriend, and that was really exciting and thrilling, but anything I shared about John was self-censored. Looking back, I wish I had shared more with friends about what I was going through.

So why did I want to go on a date night with my dad for my seventeenth birthday? I was looking to reconnect with him. Out of all the relationships that had become strained, the one with my dad had the largest divide. There was this wedge between us, and I knew full well he didn't care much for my choice in a boyfriend. It was an uncomfortable, uncommon tension I was hoping to bridge.

And you know what? We had a great time. That night is a memory I love. But I also particularly remember this night because it was when I finally got a double ear piercing and an upper cartilage piercing (very scandalous, I know), which I had been begging to get for two years.

But looking back at teenage me, I didn't know anything about men. I didn't know anything about dating. I didn't know anything about depression. And I didn't know that I didn't know anything. I was clueless. And I don't know if how my parents handled it was right. But what I do know is that they couldn't have stopped it. And now as an adult, I am very glad they kept me close during that time. They weren't going to prevent what happened, but they did prevent things from getting out of hand.

This was a tough season for me. I needed this season in my life. I needed an introduction to boys, to dating, to learning how to open up to my closest friends and family. I figured out I wanted my dad to like who I ended up with. (Fortunately, my husband was the first guy I dated whom my dad did actually like.) I also realized I could be more open with my friends. I learned to share more of myself with the two clos- est girlfriends I had at seventeen, and now at thirty-(*cough,*

cough)-something, we're still good friends to this day.

This hard season in my late teens helped define me as an adult. And I hope in sharing this, you as a parent can better understand what your child is experiencing in seasons like this. Just because I was young, I was still confronted with adult choices, feelings, and decisions, even if I wasn't ready for much of it. I still needed help. I still needed my faith, my family, and my friends even if I pushed them away. Because when everything came crashing back down, faith, family, and friends are what I returned to.

— — — — — — — — — — — — — —

Thoughts to Ponder:

- How often do you hug your children and say, "I love you"?

- The next time you have a conversation with your children, try listening more and talking less.

- Remember back to the last time your children told you something that caused alarm. Did you over-react? Decide today to extend grace and understanding when faced with challenging dilemmas.

Chapter Eleven

PARENTING WITH LOVE AND GRACE

One thing that haunted me as a mom was pondering how my children would remember me and their childhoods. Would they think back with fondness or would they shriek in horror? Occasionally, I'd be having a really good day, I mean a *really* good day, when each child seemed happy and content; I had made all the right foods; and we had played and laughed together. On those days, I'd think to myself, *Oh, my kids are so lucky; they have the best childhood; they will thank me for the mothering I provided.* But then, on the days where nothing seemed to go right—a fight breaks out with hubby in the morning, the kids are late to school, no one seems to like you, and you're pretty sure at least one of your children didn't brush their teeth while another probably slipped a giant candy bar and two snack cakes in his lunch—I'd think, *My kids are forever going to hate me; no one will come home for Christmas; and I'm certain I've damaged each beyond repair.*

Then I would think of my own parents, retired, living in Las Vegas, playing Bingo and hanging out in the casinos. When I'm on the phone with my mother, she'll start hollering at my father like this:

"Get your butt upstairs!"

"Hello. . .Mom. . .I'm still on the phone."

Talking to me now: "There's a Sonicare toothbrush on sale at Kohl's. He's gotta get going. We have a lot to do today."

"So, why does he have to go?"

"He wants to go."

Then back to my dad: "Honey, get ready, we gotta leave!"

Back to me: "Okay, I gotta go 'cause I gotta get your father's butt moving."

And she hangs up.

Growing up was very interesting to say the least.

There's a childhood birthday memory I had marked in my mind as trauma, which I just now have seen from a different light. I turned six, and my mother planned this big birthday shindig with friends and family. I remember wearing a pretty orange dress I could swirl around in and feel like a ballerina, with my black patent leather Mary Jane shoes, and a birthday crown made from orange paper with curly swigs at the top. My mother had asked me what kind of cake filling I wanted in my birthday cake. I requested pineapple. As all the kids gathered around the birthday table and my mom cut the cake, one of the kids said, "Yay banana! I love banana!" and I loved banana too, but I screamed, "Banana? I wanted pineapple!" My mother said, "The bakery didn't have pineapple filling, honey." This was not an acceptable answer for me, and I ran from the table distraught and terribly angry.

I had always seen this as one of the terrible tragedies of my childhood, but now I see it differently. My mother tried her best to make my day special. I had the dress, I had the crown, I had a big party, and at one word, *banana*, I threw a fit. I remember running to my big brother, who was out front playing with the "big kids," for comfort. I needed comfort because of smashed bananas? This was the day I learned the world wouldn't bend at my every whim and that my mother wasn't perfect. She was doing the best she could. And I hope that's how my kids see me—as a flawed human who did her best as a mother through all the really good days and not-so-good days.

LOVING IN THE DAY-TO-DAY

When my youngest was three or four years of age, he would carry around a small vial with his boogers in it. He'd proudly show them off to friends and family. One day while dropping a meal off to the youth pastor at our church (his wife had recently had foot surgery), Joey pulled out his prized booger vial and bragged about his collection. It was a bit embarrassing at first until the pastor, who was also a dad, made an endearing joke about having a collection too. Now, I know this sounds quite disgusting, and you're probably wondering why I would allow such a thing. See, the thing is, it brought my little toddler great joy, and I had bigger boogers to fry with my impossible kid, so it didn't seem worth the energy. He grew out of this, eventually—but while it lasted, it brought so much pleasure to him and great laughs for the family.

Does our children's behavior determine how good a parent

we are? Really think about that. I'm flawed, and I'm guessing you are too. And our children will be flawed, and sometimes their behavior may be frustrating, irritating, and confusing. Some days just being present will be enough. Just be present and seek love, and it will shine through on bright days, rainy days, and even through stormy days. Through permanent markers on walls to muddy dogs dragged in by muddy kids and flowerbeds destroyed by a little swordsman, at the end of your parenting trilogy, what is going to matter most? Love will be what lasts. Not things.

It's during difficult times we need to be careful that our love is not based on behavior. Love based on behavior is conditional. In fact, the more difficult children are, the more they need you and need to spend time with you. This is where many parents lose their relationship with their kids. The child becomes draining and a chore to be around, and it's easier to stay away from them. As a result, the relationship suffers and the child suffers. God doesn't stay away from us when we are difficult. When we are difficult, that's when God is closer than ever. Romans 7:24–8:1 says, "Wretched man that I am! Who will set me free from the body of this death? Thanks be to God through Jesus Christ our Lord! So then, on the one hand I myself with my mind am serving the law of God, but on the other, with my flesh the law of sin. Therefore there is now no condemnation at all for those who are in Christ Jesus." With God there is no condemnation. At all. Because of Jesus, God will never, ever condemn us. God draws us and guides us into love, truth, holiness, and usefulness. Drawing in isn't done through condemning.

PARTNER WITH THE FATHER

Parenting is a place where we make a lot of mistakes, but one mistake we do not want to make is to parent without our heavenly Father. He is always there to guide and direct us. What I did right was to cry out to God for help. As Psalm 34:17 encourages: "The righteous cry out and the LORD hears and rescues them from all their troubles." The more connected to God we are and the more we understand His love for us, the more God, as our perfect parent, can guide us to better parent our children.

When you have an impossible kid, sometimes the biggest challenge is just staying engaged and not checking out due to frustration. One day, when my daughter was a teenager, I invited her to join me: "Hey, Monica, you want to come with me and hang out and get coffee while I wait for your brother at boxing?"

"We aren't getting along right now. Why would you want me to go with you?"

"If I had stayed away from you every time we weren't getting along or you were being snotty, I would have missed half of your childhood."

This response made us both laugh, and as funny as it was, it was just as true. Like us, our children are not always pleasant. If the love we show and what we do and give as parents are conditional based on their behavior, we are not being responsible parents. The truth is our children are not always going to be pleasant to be around. . .but then neither are we!

My husband and I enjoy watching reality rescue TV shows, which include all kinds of rescues, from keeping a suicidal patient from jumping off a two-story building to helping an angry man who got punched in the nose. In one episode, there was something one of the paramedics said that really stuck with me. He said, "If they've lost any of their humanness, I haven't done my job." These professionals care for people without judgment or condemnation, and this can apply to our parenting as well.

Thinking about the passage of the prodigal son in Luke 15, the father, as a symbol of our heavenly Father, waited eagerly, was looking out for, and *ran* to his lost son. The father didn't see his prodigal son with eyes of judgment; instead, the son was embraced. In Luke 15:29–30, after celebration was underway for this "lost" son, the older son, who had stayed with his father, said, "Look! For so many years I have been serving you and I have never neglected a command of yours; and yet you never gave me a young goat, so that I might celebrate with my friends; but when this son of yours came, who has devoured your wealth with prostitutes, you slaughtered the fattened calf for him." This brother didn't see how his father saw him; he somehow thought he had to earn his father's approval and endearment through service and following commands or earning his father's love. This is not how it works with God. And this is what the father in this story was trying to convey to his older son in Luke 15:31, when he said, "Son, you have always been with me, and all that is mine is yours." The older brother's problem was that of how his father saw him.

How does God see you? Do you feel loved and embraced by God? Do you know you are a beloved and accepted child with a heavenly Father who has His arms wide open to you?

If we lose our way, we are free to return to God because He sprints out to us. When we can fully embrace and accept how God loves and receives us as His children, we are better equipped to pass that same love and acceptance on to our children.

Consider that Exodus 34:14 says, "For you shall not worship any other god, because the LORD, whose name is Jealous, is a jealous God." God cares about our relationship with Him. He is a jealous God; He desires a closeness with you—He longs for you. When we are right with God, we are right with others. God doesn't force us to do anything; He loves us as we are. God's relationship with us is what matters most to Him. He gently guides us to greater truth and greater love. It's not about rules. Our relationship with our kids needs to be centered on love, and we must move past rules and control to guide as God does.

Richard Rohr says, "The relationship God has with us is what's most important to Him. We can see this in how He forgives us over and over. It's like He's saying, 'The rules do not matter as much as My relationship with you.'" *

This parenting thing is a tough gig. If you go into motherhood with the expectation of fulfilling unmet needs, you will be gravely disappointed. On the other hand, when you enter motherhood expecting to give, give, and give, you will receive more than you ever imagined, more than your wildest dreams. And if you have an impossible kid, the journey seems infinitely more difficult.

WE SET THE PACE

In the dead of the night, while our children were sleeping, my husband would lay his hand on them and pray. He did this throughout the years they lived in our home.

When our middle child was just a tiny baby, Mike went into his room and placed his hand on his tiny body and prayed for him—falling asleep while praying. Suddenly, he and the baby were awakened by a loud bang! It was the sound of Mike's head hitting the rail on the side of the crib. As the baby screamed, Mike picked him up. Hearing the screams of the baby, I ran into the room. "What happened?"

His reply: "Don't worry about it. I got this. Go back to bed." And I did.

When Mike finally came to bed, glancing at his reflection in the mirror, he had a big red mark across his forehead.

I didn't find out what happened until twenty-four years later, when my husband told this story in a sermon. Yes, this is a funny story, but it's also a good illustration about the pace we set in our homes. Mike was covering our children in prayer. I also prayed for our kids daily. We, as parents, set the pace.

Sometimes we are the ones who start the bad attitudes in our homes. Is it possible the wrong attitude or behavior could have started with us? How did we begin our day with our kids? Were we yelling to get them up or admonishing them for something they did the night before? We set the pace. I noticed with my children, if I started the day with a smile, a hug, or an "I love you," our day went much better.

What are your words and demeanor throughout the day?

Do you sow words of encouragement? What type of tone do your children hear? Some days I would stop and think about all my words collectively in a single day. Some days went like this: *Did you brush your teeth? Don't put that there. Your room is a pigsty. Do your homework. Take out the trash. Where are you going? Stop! No. No. No.*

If you collected all the words you said to your children in one day, what would they be? Are you speaking truths into your children's lives? Are you teaching them that they were made in the image of God, who loves them and died for them? Do your words reflect how marvelously magnificent they are and that God has a plan for them?

Our children need our love and approval. They need to hear words that reflect how special they are to us and how proud we are. I know from experience how difficult this simple thing can be. There are days where it's hard enough just to keep our heads above water, let alone give out words of praise. Those are the days we need to dig deep—past nasty glares and quippy remarks—and remind ourselves that our children are special gifts from God. Try reaching deep and thinking back to the day they were born. Do you remember the first time you held your children? On the days they are snottier than usual, pull out baby pictures and remember you used to like them. You may need to do this daily if you have an impossible kid. Consider whether your children feel loved. If children don't feel loved, they are more likely to act out with anger or misbehavior.

The question *Is there anything I can help with?* can bridge misunderstanding gaps and create closeness.

TILLING THE SOIL

One evening, I persuaded Monica to take a walk with me so we could spend time talking. I knew she was in a rotten mood, but I asked her anyway. During our walk, she decided if she was miserable, she would share the "love" with me. Let's just say she was *not* showering me with compliments about what a magnificent mother I was.

The walk was a disaster, but later that night we ended up in her room talking. Perhaps had I not gone on that "lovely" walk with her, we may never have gotten to the good stuff. Sometimes you must dig through the mud to get to the treasure. Keep digging! Dig on even when there is more mud than you think you can endure.

> *Therefore, my beloved brothers and sisters, be firm, immovable, always excelling in the work of the Lord, knowing that your labor is not in vain in the Lord.*
> 1 CORINTHIANS 15:58

And then, sometimes they surprise you. As difficult as Monica was at home, when I'd see reflections of good character in her, it gave me hope. At times she would even cause me to check myself and my own character and growth. During a softball game, when Monica was about twelve, one of the other gals was having a really rough game, continually getting in the way of Monica's plays. I started feeling frustrated and whispering to my husband about my irritation. I thought to myself, *Someone needs to correct that infringing little second-base player*. At the end of a difficult inning, I saw my daughter walk over to her and I'm thinking, *Good, maybe she'll explain how this game works*, but then I saw Monica put her arm around this child and walk her to the dugout offering comfort and encouragement.

I felt like a big fat jerk.

After the game, Monica told me Kristen was having a bad day and that she felt sorry for her. I was so proud of the way she handled herself, and I praised her. Did I tell her what I had been thinking? Nope. I was too embarrassed, but I was glad my daughter's conduct gave me a needed gut check. If I could go back, I wish I had told her how she impacted me that day, but my pride got in the way.

If you want to have your pride and ego dinged, become a parent. Being a mom is a hard and often thankless job, one in which self-reflection and pulling yourself off the sticky pickle-juiced floor gives you gut checks you never imagined. And just when you're at your lowest, you'll take the kids to the park and watch another mom who seems to have it all together. This would happen for me. I'd see another mom who seemed patient, loving, and all put together—the perfect playground fashionista mom with happy kids. I just wasn't that, but I was jealous of those who were. *I'm a mess. Why can't I be like her?* I wanted to be that all-put-together mom, and I suppose on some days I might have appeared that way. The truth was, I got help from wherever I could get it. Here's what I know: most of us need help and support.

EVERY PARENT NEEDS HELP

Get help—whatever that means for you. Whether from grandparents who babysit or help guide, teachers, friends, or relatives. If someone can pour into your child something you don't have the capacity to, it's okay to reach out for whatever help you need. It doesn't diminish you or your parenting abilities; in fact, it makes you a better parent. There have been many times when I felt someone else could give Monica more of what she needed than I could.

As Monica got older, shopping trips for clothes were a doomed endeavor. I'd say things like "Too tight...too low...no way..." This usually included an argument—in the store—and ended with my proclamation that next time her dad was going to take her. When other people offered to take her shopping, I'd encourage it because she deserved to be with someone who didn't fight with her or bark at her while she was in the changing room, and that person wasn't me.

There's a memory she has about the first time I took her bra shopping. Get ready for another big fat mom fail on my part. I was thinking I'd make it really low key and try not to embarrass or cause trauma. We were out shopping as a family, and I pulled Monica aside and said, "Okay, let's find you a bra." I was thinking I was keeping it casual, not making it a "big deal." Well, it turned out to be one of the most humiliating and embarrassing experiences from her childhood memories. She remembers me saying, "Just pick something already," while her dad and brothers looked on. Pretty dense on my part, I know, but I never knew how it affected her until she was an adult. Accepting help from someone else who offered to take her shopping was a good mom move on my part because of my lack of enthusiasm for shopping.

After she was an adult and I had done some growing up myself, we went shopping, and I was helping her put outfits together. I recall her saying, "Who are you? Where were you when I was growing up?" I guess you can teach an old mom new tricks.

It's important to allow others to have an influence with our children, especially in areas where we fall short. I've already mentioned that in elementary school, our middle child, Tim, got picked on. I really didn't know what to do and reached out for help from anyone who would talk to me. Briefly meeting a female boxer, I shared my concern for my son and asked her advice. She suggested I introduce him to boxing. Tim's boxing coach, Jose, taught him things my husband and I would have never been able to teach him. Jose came from a completely different culture and background than we did, moving from Mexico to the United States at a young age. He learned to box as a way of self-preservation. The streets and a coach who was drunk most of the time were Jose's teachers. Tim was shy and timid, yet Jose took on the challenge and turned him into a fierce boxing competitor.

Jose said to me, "I gotta make this kid tough. He's too nice. He doesn't even swear, and he gets good grades. This is boxing! I gotta make him tough!" Jose developed a sense of self-confidence and fortitude in Tim that we weren't able to, and we are thankful to this day. We need to allow others to do what we can't.

Seek other adults who can come alongside you as a parent. Just because you are the parent does not mean you have all the answers. Pastors, mentors, friends, family, teachers, and coaches have all helped us raise our children. Be wise, and leverage the influence of others—especially when you have a strong-willed kid.

STRONG-WILLED
BECOMES BEAUTIFUL

When she's screaming at you and slamming doors or when he's throwing another tantrum, it's hard to imagine how this could turn into anything good—but it can in oh-so-many ways. I want to leave you with significant hope because, when you're battling with an impossible kid, some days you just want to climb under your bed and hide. Be encouraged, because struggle often turns into victory. Just like us, our children are a work in progress, and that's when God does His best work as we stay faithful and allow God's molding to transform us. Not only are we raising our children, but God is also chipping away at us and molding us to His likeness. Every struggle is an opportunity to grow, and our kids have a way of helping God mold us. Remember Philippians 1:6: "For I am confident of this very thing, that He who began a good work among you will complete it by the day of Christ Jesus."

My four-year-old grandson was protesting and not going down for his nap. Monica, feeling irritated and exhausted and needing a bit of a reprieve, hollered at him to stay in his bed. After his nap, he walked out with hands on hips and said, "Sooo, Mommy, are you going to say sorry for yelling at me?" To her credit, she did. Being a mom will mold you like nothing else can.

As God is molding us, He is also molding our children. After the rants and fits, we began to see what this type of personality becomes with understanding, steadfastness, guiding, limits, talking, and listening—struggle emerges into magnificence. Along the way, God gave us glimpses into the future as we forged through this marathon called parenting. There was one particular defining moment, the Turkey Bowl, when I felt like God wrapped me in His arms and said, "Well done, Mom."

When Monica was in junior high school, her school held the annual Turkey Bowl football game (she mentioned this game in chapter 7), where the winning team players were all awarded a frozen turkey. Monica decided she wanted to play in the Turkey Bowl in spite of the fact that most girls didn't even try out and most kids—boys and girls—didn't make the team.

She called me from school one day, over-the-moon excited. "Mom, I made the team!" She was one of two girls who had. And I cried. Not because I wanted her to play football but because she had wanted it so badly and made it happen. Her dad was pretty proud as well—what could be better than your daughter making the football team?!

The day of the game was one of my all-time highlights of motherhood. Watching her hold her own and be accepted by a team of boys was one of my proudest moments ever. Her team won, and she brought home the prized turkey.

This day was a defining moment for me as a parent. It was that day I knew she would forever be okay, knowing she could hold her own even when the odds were against her. All that obstinate behavior we saw at home, much of which was directed at me, was used in a good way. She used her determination and persistence in a productive way. She hung in there with the boys!

I am well aware that this was an odd time to feel God's presence and approval—a silly football game—but allow me to further illustrate. She followed the rules. She set a goal and achieved it. She demonstrated good sportsmanship (or sportswomanship) and character. She welcomed our presence and looked to us for celebration. She was respectful to everyone involved. And she honored God through the whole process. When you have a kid who's fighting you at every turn, you can sometimes wonder if anything you are doing is working or getting through. This day showed me our efforts were paying off.

During her high school years, there's another time that stands out too.

When Monica achieved a starting position on the varsity softball team, I was in the hospital at the start of the season. My husband had been staying overnight with me, but on this particular night, he couldn't. Monica decided she was staying. I protested, knowing she could lose her starting position she worked years to earn. I remember what she said: "Mom, I am staying overnight, and there is nothing you can do about it!" No matter what, she wasn't going to leave. She stood her ground, and that was it. Unfortunately, the coach didn't see things quite the way she did, and she lost her position. I felt horrible about it. But she shrugged it off. . .or so it seemed. Looking back, that night was one of the most special and endearing times we ever had together.

The next time your child defies you or digs their heels in under protest, stop and think, *This is good.* For it is this same tenacity they will use to stand for God, to stand up against peer pressure, and to hold their own in the world when they leave the protection of your umbrella. Stop and pray, "God, show me how to harness this for Your glory" and "Help me to see my children the way You see them."

Determined, often difficult children, when guided and directed, rise to the top and do great things. Stay the course. Look for the windows into what this type of personality becomes.

As I think about 1 Kings 2:19, after King Solomon took over the throne of his father, King David, his mother, Bathsheba, went to speak to her son. You may have missed this. I know I never noticed it until recently, but King Solomon "stood to meet her, [and] bowed to her." The king *bowed* to his mother. Can you imagine? Just for a second, think of your impossible kid giving you honor and respect. Think of this child as an adult bowing to you in honor. Now, I know our customs are different today, and I've certainly never experienced any of my children bowing to me, nor do I think this will ever happen. But in today's culture, all my kids have shown honor and respect in so many ways. For instance, my youngest son allowed me to accompany him while at Bible college in all his classes for the week I visited. My middle son, living in another state, stays connected with calls and visits, and he invites me to join his family often. My daughter welcomed my presence in the room during the birth of both of my grandchildren, and every request to visit is met with a yes. Being able to be a part of their adult lives is like bowing to me, and it's not an honor I take lightly.

CHILDREN ARE A GIFT

My joy outweighs the struggles seeing what a wonderful adult Monica turned out to be. In a fantasy world, given the choice, would I choose her to be my daughter? Absolutely! A thousand times yes! Sometimes in life what we work hardest at brings the greatest rewards. It was completely and infinitely worth every heartache along the way.

I definitely made many mistakes and became good at asking for forgiveness. You're not going to do this parenting thing perfectly. The Lord knows I've apologized to each of my kids countless times. I have discovered it's an essential part of parenting. And I ask you: Sooo, Mommy, are you going to say sorry? Please take my advice and get used to apologizing. It will free your heart, and it will open your child's heart.

Right now, you are most likely in the parenting marathon, and it may feel arduous, but eventually they leave. I remember the day Monica had all her boxes packed up in her room as she prepared to move in with her soon-to-be husband. Thinking back on the first time I held her—love consumed me, a kind of love I had never before experienced, and as suddenly as she was handed to me, she was now leaving. As she packed up her room, I questioned, *Did I pack her "luggage" with all she will need? Was I faithful as the mom God trusted me to be? She was handed to me as a gift from God, and now we are handing her off.* Emerging through the tears that day shone a thankfulness for the blessing of being able to raise her.

Even today, I wonder how she could have turned out to be such a great and godly woman even though she had a hugely flawed and slightly neurotic mother. God took a scared little girl and turned her into a mother, not a perfect one, mind you, but a good one and a loving one. What is impossible with us God makes possible. Nothing is impossible with God.

Behold, children are a gift of the L\ORD,
the fruit of the womb is a reward.
PSALM 127:3

Parenting is a journey that none of us really knows how to travel. We go along our path, not sure which fork to take or which hill to climb, and along the way we get stuck in a few ditches. All anyone can ever do is give it your best shot. When we look back, we can be satisfied if we can say, "I did my best." Enjoy this journey, my friend, and remember to slow down and dance with your kids and pause to enjoy and delight in your children's presence.

My prayer for you is Proverbs 31:28: "Her children rise up and bless her." There is no greater joy for a mother.

One more thing. . .

Well done, Mom, well done!

— — — — — — — — — — — —

THOUGHTS FROM MONICA:

I'm not going to share much here because all that wisdom, from all her years (not an age joke), really sums it all up quite wonderfully. But like many of you who are reading this book, I assume you are in a similar position to mine: we're in the thick of it. Some days you're crossing that finish line like Rocky at the top of the stairs. Other days—many other days—you're just that mom in yoga pants and greasy hair, eating the leftover chicken nuggets from a four-year-old's plate, thankful you got a meal in today. So, when my mother describes me as a "great and godly" woman, I can't help but chuckle between my nugget-filled cheeks.

But like you, I'm working on it. I'm doing my best. And the journey you're on with your strong-willed child may look a little different than the one my mother and I had, but you're working on it. And that type of tough, hard, sometimes painful work as a parent does not return fruitless.

— — — — — — — — — — — —

Thoughts to Ponder:

- Do you know how much God loves you and accepts you? Do you know how special you are to your heavenly Father? Remember that His arms are always open to you.

- Find ways to express to your children how much you love spending time with them and how you delight in their presence.

- When faced with where to invest your time, ask yourself, "Who needs me more?"

- Would you consider starting a mom group using this book as a guide for discussions? Every mom can benefit from support and camaraderie.

*Richard Rohr, *Falling Upward* (San Francisco: Jossey-Bass, 2011): 56–57 [paraphrase].

About the Author

— — — — — — — — — —

Lucille Williams, national speaker and author, has ministered to couples and families for more than twenty-five years. As a pastor's wife, Lucille dedicates her time to ministry, writing, mentoring, and providing resources on her blog at LuSays .com. Working alongside her husband, who is the children's pastor at Palmcroft Church in Phoenix, Arizona, Lucille found widespread success with her first book, *From Me to We*, followed by *The Intimacy You Crave*.

In her pursuit to safeguard marriages, Lucille has appeared on *Focus on the Family's* radio broadcasts and magazine as one of their top-rated programs for "BEST OF 2018." She was also featured on KKLA's the *Frank Sontag Show* and GOD TV. Even with her writing and speaking achievements, she will tell you her greatest pride and joy is her family—her highest calling and ministry.

Lucille and her husband of more than thirty-eight years reside in Peoria, Arizona, where they spend the majority of their spare time with their grandkids.

OTHER BOOKS BY LUCILLE WILLIAMS

From Me to We
A Premarital Guide for the Bride- and Groom-to-Be

Here's a transparent, surprisingly honest, and widely informative guide that will inspire readers to safeguard their marriage by tackling tough questions and issues before they say, "I do." Lucille Williams offers straight-talk about marriage with unprecedented insight as well as challenges and discussion questions—a great tool for premarital counseling.

Paperback / 978-1-63409-863-2 / $14.99

The Intimacy You Crave
Straight Talk about Sex and Pancakes

Within the pages of *The Intimacy You Crave* are relatable, real-life fantasies and desires of everyday women—but more important are the step-by-step instructions and straight-talk about sex from a pastor's wife that will challenge and equip readers to work toward a greater intimacy that infiltrates every area of married life.

Paperback / 978-1-64352-060-5 / $14.99